The Promised Land

The Story of Emigration
from Oxfordshire, and Neighbouring
Buckinghamshire, Northamptonshire and
Warwickshire 1815-1914

Captain James Cook wearing full captain's full-dress uniform, 1774-1787, by Nathaniel Dance. (National Maritime Museum).

Also written by Martin Greenwood

Villages of Banburyshire *including Lark* Rise to Candleford Green
In Flora's Footsteps, Daily Life in Lark Rise Country, 1876-2009
Pilgrim's Progress Revisited, The Nonconformists of Banburyshire, 1662-2012
The Real Candleford Green, The Story of a Lark Rise Village

The Promised Land

The Story of Emigration from Oxfordshire, and Neighbouring Buckinghamshire, Northamptonshire and Warwickshire 1815-1914

Martin Greenwood (signature)

MARTIN GREENWOOD

Published by
Robert Boyd Publications
260 Colwell Drive, Witney
Oxfordshire OX28 5LW

ISBN: 978 1 908738 40 0

First published 2020

Printed in the United Kingdom
by Henry Ling Limited
at the Dorset Press
Dorchester DT1 1HD

Contents

	List of Tables and Illustrations	8
	Foreword and Acknowledgements	11
Chapter 1	Captain Cook, Transportation and Penal Colonies	13
Chapter 2	Major Emigrant Settlements	17
Chapter 3	Social Unrest and Poor Law Problems	23
Chapter 4	Emigration from Oxfordshire and neighbouring Buckinghamshire, Northamptonshire and Warwickshire, 1815-1850	27
Chapter 5	The Victorian Empire, Agricultural Depressions and Trade Unionism	55
Chapter 6	The Great Exodus, 1850-1914	67
Chapter 7	Migrant Ports, Shipping and Passages	85
Chapter 8	Diaries and Other Records of Emigrants	107
Chapter 9	Conclusion	117
	Epilogue	119
Appendix 1	List of Oxfordshire Emigrants Lost in the Wreck of the *Cataraqui*, 1845.	121
Appendix 2	The Durham Report	123
Appendix 3	Cornish Emigration	127
	Bibliography	129
	Notes	131
	Index	135

Cover illustrations

Front: *'The Last of England'*, by Ford Madox Brown, 1855
(Birmingham Museums and Art Galleries).

Back: *'The Parting Cheer'*, by Henry Nelson O'Neil, 1861
(National Maritime Museum).

Tables

1. Timeline, 1760-1914.   10
2. Population Growth in Oxfordshire, 1801-1911.   31
3. Population in Oxfordshire, 1801-1911.   32
4. Population in Buckinghamshire, 1801-1911.   40
5. Population in Northamptonshire, 1801-1911.   43
6. Population in Warwickshire, 1801-1911.   51
7. Return of Owners of Land in the Four Shires, 1873.   69
8. Emigrant Ships used by the Four Shires, 1823-1912.   93

Illustrations

Captain James Cook, 1774-1787, by Nathaniel Dance. 3

Map of Australia. 19

Map of New Zealand 21

Map of Oxfordshire and Neighbouring Shires. 31

John George Lambton, 1st Earl of Durham, by Charles Turner, 1831. 56

Map of Upper and Lower Canada, 1837-38. 57

'Cutty Sark' in Sydney Harbour, 1885-1894. 58

'SS Great Britain', Bristol, 1843. 59

Emigration to Queensland with Mr E.Richardson, official notice, 1873. 63

Nonconformist Finger Post, Sheffield, Tasmania. 65

Map of Northern Queensland, Australia. 74

Canning Dock and the Customs House, Liverpool, 1860s. 87

Liverpool from the Pier Head, c.1906. 87

The "Three Graces", Liverpool, 1920s. 88

'1913 Setting Sail for a Better Life a World Away – Liverpool to Australia.' 88

' Darling Downs', Gravesend Reach, River Thames, 1852. 94

'Cospatrick', Gravesend Reach, River Thames, 1856. 94

'Ramsey', Gravesend Reach, River Thames, 1863. 95

'Victoria' entering New York Harbour. 95

'Constance', built 1848. 96

'Hankow', Gravesend Reach, River Thames, 1873. 96

'Demosthenes', Gravesend Reach, River Thames, 1911. 97

'R.M.S. Titanic', 1912. 97

Sydney Harbour in late 19th century. 98

'The Emigrant Ship' by Charles Joseph Staniland (1838-1916), late 1880s. 100

Emigrants at dinner on a migration ship, 14 April 1844. 100

Burning of the Emigrant Ship Ocean Monarch, 24 August 1848. 102

The Cataraqui cairn, King Island, Australia, unveiled 2 August 2020. 103

Crossing the Murray River, North Queensland, the Butler family, c.1910. 111

Picnic Aussie Style, Outback, Northern Queensland, the Butler family, c.1910. 111

Fringford Working Party, Northern Queensland, the Butler family, c.1910. 112

Thomas, Henry and Charles Butler, Magnetic Island, Northern Queensland, early 1920s. 113

Fringford Farm, Murray Upper, Northern Queensland, 1920s. 113

Table 1
Timeline 1760-1914

1760 George III's accession
1768 Captain Cook's first voyage to the Pacific on *Endeavour*
1776 Start of the American War of Independence
1787 First Fleet to Australia
1788 First transportation to New South Wales
1790 French Revolution
1793 France declares war
c.1795 'Speenhamland Treatment' of the poor introduced in Berkshire
1815 Battle of Waterloo & End of the Napoleonic Wars
1815 Corn Laws
1819 'Peterloo Massacre', Manchester
1820 George IV
1825 Repeal of anti-trade union legislation
1829 Catholic Emancipation
1830-31 Swing Riots
1830 William IV
1831 Swing Riots
1832 Reform Bill
1832 Cholera epidemic probably killed 31,000.
1834 Poor Law Amendment Act
1837 Queen Victoria
1839 Newport Protest- 14 killed and others transported to Tasmania.
1841 New Penny Post
1845-50 Irish Potato Famine, about one million died of malnutrition, and 2 million
    emigrated between 1845 and 1855.
1846 Repeal of the Corn Laws
1846 Durham Report accepted- sets future relationships with the colonies.
1851 The Great Exhibition. The Great Exodus starts.
1851 Agriculture accounted for 20.3% of the national income
1853-56 Crimean War
1868-74 The Boom Years
1872 National Agricultural Labourers Union (Joseph Arch)
1874-85 Agricultural Depression — first wave
1884 Agricultural labourers get the vote
1891-96 Second wave of Agricultural Depression
1893 New County Councils, then Parish & District Councils
1893 New Labour Party (Keir Hardie) founded
1897 Queen Victoria's Diamond Jubilee
1899-1902 The Boer War.
1901 Edward VII
1901 Agriculture accounted for only 6.4% of the national income
1906 Liberal land slide, Labour Party gained 30 seats.
1908 Old Age Pension Scheme
1910 George V
1908 Labour Unrest- 10 million strike days
1910-11 Series of major strikes, including the first general railway strike (1911)
1911 Lloyd George's National Insurance Bill 1913 Over 4 million Union members
1914-18 First World War

Foreword and Acknowledgements

For many years I have researched, written and talked about changes in village life in the late 19th century, particularly in relation to Flora Thompson's Lark Rise villages, Juniper Hill, Cottisford and Fringford in Oxfordshire. The decline in village populations in this period was very marked, mainly due to the agricultural depressions of the 1870s and 1890s, and to foreign competition. This led to migration to the northern industrial cities and significantly to emigration, particularly to the United States, Canada, Australia and New Zealand. Between 1853 and 1913, some 13 million emigrated, most of them farm labourers. Many of them saw it as a search for 'The Promised Land', and land was often on offer in the colonies. I have always been interested in emigration, given the number of my ancestors who ended up in various parts of the world and my own experience of living in West Africa, the United States and Canada. However, it was my contact with one old Fringford family, the Butlers, which inspired me to look at emigration in more detail, as four brothers emigrated to Northern Queensland in the early 1870s. A chance meeting in Fringford churchyard with two Butler descendents from Australia led to an extended correspondence with various members of the family and a wealth of information and documentation from them about the family's experience in Australia from the 1870s.

Emigration is a vast subject, given the numbers and the different countries involved, and it is certainly over ambitious for me to attempt a comprehensive study. The records are kept in a variety of places and are not always easy to access, particularly as the best ones are often abroad. I have, therefore, limited my detailed coverage to Oxfordshire, with supporting evidence from neighbouring Buckinghamshire, Northamptonshire and Warwickshire. Oxfordshire, as a rural county, experienced one of the highest levels of emigration, and the populations of most of its villages stagnated after 1871. Given the special Fringford connection with Northern Queensland, I have concentrated on emigration to Australia and New Zealand, rather than the United States, which is a vast subject in its own right.

In Chapter 1, I look at the voyages of Captain Cook, transportation and penal colonies. In Chapter 2, I provide details of the major emigrant settlements. In Chapter 3, I discuss social unrest and Poor Law problems prior to the Reform Bill of 1832 and the Poor Law Act of 1834. In Chapter 4, I examine emigration from the four shires, 1815 -1850. In Chapter 5, I look at the growth of the Victorian Empire, together with the agricultural depressions, trade unionism, and the

Nonconformists. In Chapter 6, I examine the Great Exodus, 1850-1914 and its effect on the four shires. In Chapter 7, I investigate the experience of the emigrants at the migrant ports, like Liverpool, the famous emigrant paintings and at their costs, shipping, passages and epidemic diseases. In Chapter 8, I take a look at some diaries and other records of emigrants. In the epilogue I recall some of the emigration of my own family.

I would like to offer a special thank you to members of the Butler family, including Joan Goodin and Grace Rutherford, who are sadly no longer with us, and Rhonda Smith and Pat Spence, who have all shared their memories, photographs and research into the family in Northern Queensland. I would like to thank members of the Whitton family and Margaret and Eric Smith for sharing their memories and research into their families. I am very grateful to Jeremy Gibson for his work on the Poor Law emigrants from the Banbury Poor Law Union. I would like to thank Jeremy Coke-Smyth for his information about Lord Durham's time in Canada in 1839, and Des Café for the wealth of information which he has provided from Australia. I am grateful to Catherine Lorigan for her expertise on Cornish emigration. I would like to thank the staff of the Oxfordshire History Centre (OHC) for their patience and assistance in answering my queries; also the staff of the Centre for Buckingham-shire Studies (CBS), the Northamptonshire Record Office (NRO), and the Warwickshire County Record Office (WCRO) for their assistance. I am also very grateful to the staff of the Tasmania Record Office and the Queensland Record Office for their assistance. I also owe a special thank you to Roger Hull for the Liverpool City Council (LCC) and Scarlet Faro at the National Maritime Museum (NMM) for their patience and assistance and allowing me to use some of their photographs.

I am very grateful to Julie Barrett for drawing the excellent maps. I am hugely indebted to Bob Boyd for all his assistance and advice in publishing this book. I would also like to offer a special thank you to Marilyn Yurdan for her rigorous but kindly reading of the text; her suggestions led to significant improvements in the text and presentation. Finally, a very special thank you to Anne for her infinite patience while I have been researching and writing this book.

Martin Greenwood
Fringford, September 2020

Chapter 1

Captain Cook, Transportation and Penal Colonies

Captain Cook

In looking at the story of emigration, it is hard to over-emphasise the importance of the voyages of Captain James Cook, which brought a whole new understanding of Australasia and the South Pacific. They also led directly to the subsequent emigrant settlements in Australia and New Zealand. Cook first set sail on the *Endeavour* in 1768, in command of the first scientific expedition to the Pacific. Ostensibly the object of the voyage was to observe the transit of the planet Venus across the Sun at Tahiti in June 1769. However, he was also given a sealed packet of instructions to verify the existence of the Great Southern Continent, an imagined land mass that cartographers felt must exist south of the equator in order to balance the globe. If he found land he was 'to cultivate a Friendship and Alliance' with its inhabitants, to chart its coastline and to assess its potential as a source of trading goods. He was also instructed to 'take possession of Convenient Situations in the Country in the name of the King of Great Britain', with the consent of the inhabitants. How this was to be done, in the absence of shared language, laws and economic systems, was open to question!

The Admiralty hoped that this vast, undiscovered continent would be rich in gold and spices. During this voyage, which finished in 1771, and his next, from 1772-75, not only did he dispel the myth of the Great Southern Continent, but he charted virtually the entire Pacific basin, bringing back detailed observations of everything he and his crew encountered. This included a complete chart of New Zealand and landings at Botany Bay (later Sydney), northern Queensland and on Possession Island, on the northern tip of Australia, where he claimed the whole east coast of Australia for King George II1. This was all that those interested in new settlements for emigrants could have wanted. As Cook's biographer, Vanessa Colingridge; has said 'To think that he did that back in the 18th century in a wooden ship and without a map – three times crossing the Antarctic – is quite extraordinary.'[i]

Transportation to America

Beginning in the seventeenth century and for 150 years afterwards, thousands were sent to the American colonies forcibly, as punishment for their lawbreaking. It is estimated that some 50,000 men, women and children were transported to

America and the West Indies between 1614 and 1775.[ii] Most were from the poorest class and nearly half were sentenced in courts in the London area. Transportation was not simply a matter of dumping them on the colonies: the aim was for the convict to be forced to learn good work habits of industry and self-discipline, while at the same time benefiting the development of the colonial economy. Usually it was the young who were transported, as they were the most likely to benefit from a new life in a new world and be fit enough to provide productive labour. Although transportation to North America ceased with the outbreak of the American War of Independence in 1776, sentences of transportation were still passed. It should also be noted that the bulk of emigration across the Atlantic related to free emigration not transportation.

Penal Colonies in Australasia
The American prisons rapidly became overcrowded, overflowing into old ships' hulks moored in coastal waters. The solution was to develop a new penal colony, and Captain Cook had provided the obvious solution. It also seems clear that England was seeking to prevent a French colonial empire from expanding into Australasia. In 1787, the First Fleet of eleven ships set sail for Botany Bay on the east coast of Australia. A second fleet followed in 1790 and a third left in 1791. In 1788, a penal colony was established at Port Jackson, New South Wales (NSW), which led to Australia becoming the focus of transportation, although the penal settlements were limited to NSW, Van Diemen's Land (VDL) and Norfolk Island. New Zealand was part of Australia until 1840 but it was never used as a penal colony. In 1805, there was a move by the Government to require all persons to move from Norfolk Island to VDL with goods and livestock. The offer of larger areas in VDL was not successful, but sterner measures led to 554 persons moving with 356 separate grant deeds by 1808. Most grants were less than 40 acres but some people were given much larger areas if they had prospered on Norfolk Island. In 1825, VDL was proclaimed a separate colony from NSW.

From 1788 to 1840, some 80,000 English convicts were transported to NSW, with the greatest number between 1821 and 1831. Following the suspension of transportation to NSW in 1840, all convicts were sent to VDL which handled some 70,000 convicts (1803-53) or about 40% of all those sent to Australia. Most difficult ones were sent to the Tasman Peninsula prison at Port Arthur. Female convicts were assigned as servants for free settlers or sent to a 'female factory' that is a women's workhouse prison; there were five of them in VDL. In 1824, Queensland's first penal colony was started at Moreton Bay (later Brisbane). In the 1830s, 4,000 people were being transported every year, with a further 9,500 male convicts transported to Western Australia from 1850 to 1853.[iii] The last convict ship to VDL arrived in 1848, and on 1 January 1856, VDL was renamed

Tasmania, and 'no longer a by-word for vice and hopelessness'.[iv] In 1857, transportation was effectively abolished, although the Home Secretary retained the right to impose transportation for specific offences until 1868. Overall estimates suggest that more than 1,000 ships transported 162,000 men, women and children to Australia between 1787 and 1867.

Below are two examples of local men who were transported as convicts.

John and Reuben Butler of Stoke Lyne, Oxon

On 6 March 1827, at Oxford Assizes, John Butler, son of Matthias and Ann Gilbert, and his son, Reuben, were both convicted of 'burglariously breaking open a barn of John Borton at Stoke Lyne, with intent to steal a quantity of chaff, value 1s.6d'. The death sentence was commuted to life and in all 19 convicted men were transported from Oxford to the *Justitia* Hulk at Woolwich on 2 May 1827. They were transported on 28 May to the *Prince Regent* which sailed from Deal on 11 June. It arrived in Sydney on 27 September 1827. As a prisoner, John worked as a labourer and woodcutter at the Australian Agriculture Company, Port Stephens. On the recommendation of Patrick's Plains Bench he was given a Ticket of Leave Passport on 22 February 1839. He died 9 July 1845, at Whittingham, NSW. As a prisoner, Reuben worked as a ploughman at Fordwich for John Blaxland, Patrick's Plains, near Broke. On the application of Mr Blaxland, he was pardoned on 1 October 1842. On 16 May 1842, at St Andrew's Church, Singleton, NSW, he married Mary Hyson, who was born in 1827, in NSW. They had 12 children.[v] He died on 13 January 1869 at Broke, NSW.

The original death sentence for attempted theft of chaff seems extraordinary to us today but it was in a time of great social unrest, as we shall see in Chapter 3.

The Terry Family of Tingewick, Bucks

Richard Terry (the elder), Richard Terry (the younger) and Joseph Terry of Tingewick were convicted at Aylesbury Assizes on 9 March 1844 and sentenced to transportation for life for aiding and abetting the rape of Ann Pepper. They all arrived at Norfolk Island on board the *Agincourt* on 9 November 1844. The regime at Norfolk Island had been much less inhumane from 1840 to 1844, under the Commandant Alexander McConochie, a prison expert and reformer. However, when the Terrys arrived in late 1844 the system had reverted to its former brutality. In 1847, they were transferred to VDL, and received a Conditional Pardon in 1856. Richard (the elder), aged 47, married Jane Stanbrook, aged 46, at the Perth Church on 30 June 1853. Richard (the younger), aged 28, married Mary Ann Baulch, aged 16, at the Perth Church on 27 December 1855. Joseph vanished from Tasmania in the early 1860s and may have gone to New Zealand, where a man of the corresponding age and county of birth died in Dunedin in 1876. It is worth noting that a series of some 21 letters from the two Richards have survived, and these show that they both did well enough to send some money back to their relatives in England.[vi]

These men were exposed to the most brutal of regimes, both on the Australian mainland and on Norfolk Island and VDL However, they survived and managed to live relatively normal lives after their release, no doubt a better life than they would have had in England at the time.

Chapter 2

Major Emigrant Settlements

North America

As noted already, the bulk of migration across the Atlantic related to free emigrants not transportation. Between 1660 and 1700, some 100,000 to 150,000 started a new life in America, which they saw as the 'Land of Promise'.[vii] Overall, it is estimated that since 1607 over 10 million emigrants have left Great Britain and Ireland for the USA, with 4 million going to Canada. From 1815 to 1850 Canada was the primary destination of English emigrants, although many who went there initially moved on to the USA. Prior to 1840, 983,227 left the UK, of whom the bulk went to North America, while 58,449 went to Australia and New Zealand. Between 1845 and 1851, when Ireland suffered a Potato Famine, about 700,000 died and over 1.25 million emigrated to the USA, with a quarter of a million leaving in 1851 alone. There was also a huge number of Irish emigrant deaths, some 20,000 dying in Canada in 1847, of whom 5,424 died from disease, mainly cholera, and are commemorated at the Quarantine (Q) Station on Grosse Ile in the Gulf of St Lawrence. In total in 1852, 277,134 crossed the Atlantic, and between 1846 and 1855, 2,740,000 left Great Britain and Ireland. Most settled in North America, while some 430,000 went to Australia, New Zealand or South Africa.

Canada

The Canada Act 1791 created representative assemblies for the two new provinces of Upper and Lower Canada. Upper Canada was largely British, and Lower Canada French. In the Canada Act 1840, which embodied some of the proposals in the Durham Report (see Chapter 5 and Appendix 2), Upper and Lower Canada were united. In 1867 the British North America Act gave Canada federal and almost wholly self-governing Dominion status. The settlement of British Columbia really began with the Gold Rush of the 1860s, although Fort Victoria was established on Vancouver Island in 1843. The provinces of Alberta and Saskatchewan were established in 1905. The Northwest Territories were the residue of the extensive domain of the Hudson's Bay and North West Companies, which were governed directly from Ottawa until 1951.

Australia

As noted already, in 1788 New South Wales (NSW) was founded as a penal colony, and it originally comprised over half of the Australian mainland, New Zealand and VDL. Later, there were separate colonies of settlement in VDL (1803), Western Australia (Swan River Colony 1828), South Australia (1836), Victoria (1851) and Queensland, which was only separated from New South Wales to become a colony in 1859. New Zealand was also treated as part of Australia until 1841. Northern Territory was excised from South Australia in 1911. In the 1840s, Edward Gibbon Wakefield introduced planned settlement in Australia and New Zealand - his settlers went out as complete communities, with the trades and professions represented.[viii] In 1842, free settlement was allowed, and in 1848 the first free immigrant ship, the *Artemisia*, arrived in Moreton Bay (later Brisbane). In 1851, the new state of Victoria was finally separated from NSW and granted responsible government. The name of the new state was said to have been chosen by Queen Victoria herself. The following year became a turning point for the new state, indeed for the whole of Australia. The drought ended, new grass sprang up in the burnt out areas, and the losses in sheep and cattle were to a large extent made up. Then came news of the discovery of gold in Bathurst, NSW and in Ballarat and Bendigo, Victoria. Ballarat was some 70 miles west of Melbourne, and within a few days Melbourne became almost deserted as everyone flocked to Ballarat. This created a Gold Rush, with most diggers coming from England and Scotland. As the news reached the outside world, every vessel was crowded with would–be gold seekers. At the same time, the invention of the steam engine, leading to the introduction of steamships, reduced voyages to Australia to 80 days.

Until then trade with Australia was not important, given that emigrant ships were small, badly manned and slow, and in many cases little better than floating coffins. So bad were conditions that in 1844 a Parliamentary Committee was set up to enquire into complaints. The shipyards in Glasgow and Aberdeen then began producing larger ships which became famous in the Australian and Far East trade, carrying wool and hides on return voyages after landing emigrants, or loading tea from China. Iron vessels gradually replaced wooden ones. In 1851, the total population of Victoria was about 77,000. Six years after, it rose to over 400,000, and by 1874 Melbourne was 'a great and prosperous city'.[ix] Its population had been swelled by the influx of disillusioned gold-diggers. After its separation in 1859, Queensland was especially active in encouraging emigrants, partly because it was tainted by convict transportation and had to try hard to attract people to a more distant colony. In 1860, Henry Jordan was appointed the new colony's agent and his work included offering land grants to those who paid the full fees and free passages to poorer emigrants. The most curious migrants were

Map of Australia
(Julie Barrett)

the groups of young women who, carefully chaperoned and segregated, went out in batches to the colonies. The Queensland Government ran an official scheme for such Female Emigrants. Their passages were paid, and jobs were guaranteed for them, so long as they could prove themselves healthy, of good character, and more or less the right age. Every month, the British India boat to Brisbane carried eighty or a hundred of them, under the care of a matron and two under-matrons. Presumably these women were potential wives.

In 1858 and 1872, new laws were passed to free up land in all the six Australian colonies. People could select a plot, buy it at auction, after which they had to live on it for a year and make improvements to it. In the 1870s and 1880s there was a booming economy and much successful emigration. On 1 January, 1901, the six Australian colonies were federated and became a Dominion. In 1926, the Balfour Declaration recognized all Dominions as 'autonomous Communities within the British Empire', and in 1931 the Statute of Westminster confirmed the full legislative independence of the Dominions.

On a lighter note, in 1861 Anglo-Australian cricket started with Isambard Brunel's *SS Great Britain* 'the ship that changed the world' sailing from Liverpool to Sydney with the England Cricket Team led by Heathfield Stephenson. The voyage took 66 days via Cape Town where they had to refuel with coal. As for the standard of Australian cricket, Roger Iddison of Yorkshire, one of the original voyagers on the Great Britain, said: 'Oi doant think mooch of [the Australians'] play, but they are a wonderful lot of drinking men'. The next tours were in 1863 and then 1873-74, led by WG Grace, who held out for the enormous fee of £1,500, plus all he could eat and drink (vast quantities).[x]

New Zealand

As noted, New Zealand was never used as a penal colony. In 1838, the French whaling Captain, Jean Langlois, landed with his ship, the *Cachelet*, at Akaroa, the 'Long Harbour', off Christchurch on the South Island. He returned in 1840 with 60 settlers on the *Comte de Paris* to found a French colony. In 1840, under the Treaty of Waitangi, the British Government acquired sovereignty over the whole country by agreement with a number of Maori chiefs. In 1841, New Zealand was detached from Australia and became a colony within the British Empire. In 1856, it became self-governing. In 1843 the colony of Canterbury was conceived, as one of several settlements planned by Edward Wakefield, as noted above, and was one of two that were deliberately denominational. The Canterbury Association was founded in London in March 1848, and recruited settlers from southern England. In the 1860s, most migrants settled in the South Island due to gold discoveries and available flat grass for pastoral farming. The Otago colony was Church of Scotland, and Dunedin, its capital, was to remain Scottish to its core for ever. The Canterbury settlement was Anglican (or High Anglican) for the Oxford Movement was reaching its peak in England.[xi] In 1851, within six months of the first four ships landing in Christchurch, they were playing cricket in Hagley Park. The old wooden pavilion, which served in 1864 when English cricketers first played in Christchurch, is next to the new one.[xii]

In June 1859, the White Star Line sent its first ship, the *Tornado*, to Auckland and Wellington, New Zealand, with 285 passengers, and a promise of free grants of 40 acres for each family. The *Mermaid* followed in July, with further monthly passages planned. In 1861, emigration to New Zealand escalated with the discovery of gold, and the population rocketed from 99,000 in 1861 to 256,000 in 1871. From the 1870s onwards, the New Zealand Government, dominated by Sir Julius Vogel, the Colonial Treasurer and soon to be Prime Minister, authorised the colony's first major public work projects to build roads and railways. These required a large number of labourers, mainly from England and Northern Europe, who were given assisted passage, with as many as 46,000 arriving in 1874

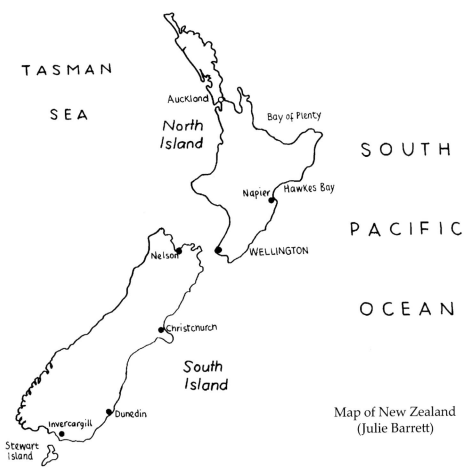

Map of New Zealand
(Julie Barrett)

and 100,000 in 1871-1880. Vogel travelled to London to negotiate loans and concluded an agreement with J.Brogden and Son to construct railways and provide plant to the value of £500,000. Brogdens had been very successful rail contractors but as rail construction was coming to an end in the UK they were looking for contracts overseas. In 1872, they were awarded six rail contracts in New Zealand. For this privilege they had to pay the government £10 per adult and could take promissory notes from the adult immigrants not exceeding £16 each.

The government started its own immigration programme and it also made an agreement with Brogdens that they would dispatch up to 2,000 able-bodied men plus wives and children to a maximum of 6,000 adults, known as the Brogdenites or the Brogden Navvies. The company was offering better terms than the New Zealand government, so the colony's Agent-General in London, Dr Isaac Featherstone, directed staff to support Brogdens' programme. Charles Carter (1822-96), a member of Featherstone's recruitment staff who interviewed nearly all the 'Brogden navvies', had been a Chartist sympathizer and an active propagandist for improved working class conditions before emigrating to New Zealand in 1850 and the campaign worked closely with the unions. It was Carter who held the meetings in the Wychwoods in 1872-73 (see Chapters 5 and 6).[xiii]

South Africa

The British took South Africa from the Dutch in 1795. Immigration began mostly after 1820 when a group of 3,695 British subjects settled in Eastern Cape Province. 90,000 applied, of whom only this number were approved, and they arrived in about 60 parties. There was serious unemployment in Britain then, so many applicants were poor. But they were encouraged by the Cape government to boost the English speaking population to offset the Xhosa peoples. They were granted farms but many lacked agricultural experience, so withdrew to Bathurst, Grahamstown, East London and Port Elizabeth, where typically they reverted to their trades. In 1845-51, 4,000 plus arrived, and in 1854 the Cape was granted its first government.

Between 1857 and 1867, some 12,000 arrived in South Africa. In 1873-75, the Revd Thomas Fuller (1831-1910), the Cape Emigrant Agent, from his Colonial Street office in the City of London, recruited 3,300. He was a far from ordinary emigration agent, trained as a third-generation Baptist minister, a Baptist pastor in three English counties, and his grandfather, the Revd Andrew Fuller, had been a 'famous Baptist preacher and theologian'. The Revd Thomas Fuller had recently been a newspaper editor in Cape Town, and he was to become a prominent Cape politician. He was now writing his 'Report on Immigration and Labour Supply for 1875' for the Cape Parliament. The current wave of immigration ended in 1878, to be followed by the Cape's final instalment in 1880-85 when 4,652 came in one year alone. In 1874-1900, more than 30,000 settlers came to Cape Town from Britain and mainland Europe. Gold was discovered in the 1850s and there was a minor gold rush in 1874 but diamond fever had gripped from 1867. Mention should be made here of the significant number of Cornishmen, with their mining skills, who emigrated here, particularly from the 1870s. In the 30 years 1870-1901, South Africa's white population more than quadrupled to over a million. In terms of red tape, the Revd Fuller found that he could not send someone to the Cape unless there was 'an order they would satisfy'. It took time to satisfy the aided emigration regulations and raise the money for a deposit, and the processes were 'not infrequently misunderstood'.[xiv] The Union of South Africa was formed in 1910 and included the two formerly self-governing British Colonies of Cape Colony (self-governed since 1872) and Natal (self-governed since 1893), together with the former Boer Republics of Transvaal and the Orange Free State, which had secured self-government in 1907.

Chapter 3

Social Unrest and Poor Law Problems

Social Unrest

The Napoleonic wars from 1793 to 1815 kept a rein on social unrest but afterwards there were immediate problems for the government. In particular, there were some explicit revolutionary ideas of some leaders of the working classes. The landed gentry pressed for, and obtained, the maintenance of subsidy on grain through the Corn Laws of 1815. These protected the landed gentry following the collapse of the artificially high prices caused by the Napoleonic wars. They also probably staved off for over a decade discontent among farm workers, although the price of bread, kept higher than it might have been, made post-war adjustment more difficult. However, farm workers were by their nature more conservative, and averse to change, than the workers in the new industrial towns, where the end of the post-war boom caused widespread unemployment and a fall in wages. It was there that the threat to order came and the Home Office under its repressive head, Viscount Sidmouth, and his local agents cowed agitators, but at a price.

The flash-point came in Manchester on 16 August 1819, when a crowd of 50-60,000 gathered at St Peter's Fields, Manchester, to hear Orator Hunt speak on Parliamentary Reform. The crowds were orderly but the local magistracy panicked and ordered the yeomanry to arrest Hunt and disperse the assembly. The soldiers turned on the crowd and nine men and two women were killed and about 400 wounded. Within days, the term 'Peterloo' (a play on Waterloo) came to signify the horror, disgust and fury of the Radical commons for their so-called superiors.[xv] This led to further outbreaks in the following year, notably the 'Cato Street conspiracy' to assassinate the Cabinet in London. Repression – the gallows and transportation- was sharp and effective, but in the long term it strengthened resistance and steadily discredited the government. In 1819, Lord Liverpool's ministry, alarmed by the unrest, passed the Six Acts, which prohibited meetings of more than 50 people, increased stamp duties on newspapers, made the publication of blasphemous and seditious libels a transportable offence, and extended the summary powers of Justices of the Peace.[xvi]

It became clear that these measures were too repressive and in 1825 the Foreign Office repealed the Six Acts and anti-trade legislation. Only Parliamentary reform remained to be implemented, and this was regarded by some as equivalent to treachery. Before the Reform Bill of 1832 the House of Commons consisted of burgesses elected by towns, knights of the shire elected by counties and representatives elected by the universities. In the counties large tenant farmers were excluded from the franchise unless they had a freehold estate worth 40 shillings or more per annum. In 1830, the 'Swing Riots' were provoked by the failure of the harvest of 1829 and the widespread introduction of threshing-machines but they were also the product of overpopulation and under-employment and the economy. The 'Captain Swing' riots were mostly in southern England but also in the Midlands and East Anglia. Hayricks and barns were burnt, machines destroyed and unpopular Poor Law officials attacked. Riots were spontaneous and without central direction. The savage official response between November 1830 and March 1831 saw 1,400 rioters brought before the courts, and resulted in 9 executions, 657 imprisoned and 464 transported but in southern England at least the introduction of the labour-saving threshing machine was considerably delayed. In Oxfordshire, there were riots on Otmoor, in Iffley, and the Oxford Bread Riots.

When the Reform Bill was initially rejected by the Lords, well-organised 'Political Unions' held massive rallies in the cities; rioters attacked Nottingham Castle and, worst of all, in Bristol the Bishop's Palace and the Mansion House were burned down, houses and shops looted, and the prisoners set free from the gaol.[xvii] In April 1832, the Lords gave way on the Reform Bill – by nine votes - much to the relief of Grey's government considering their savage response to the Swing Riots. Fifty-six 'pocket' boroughs (where seats were at the disposal of a patron or group of patrons) in England were disenfranchised, thirty were reduced to one member only, and twenty-two new boroughs were created to send two members and twenty to send one member. However, for years thereafter the political equilibrium effectively remained the same as it had ever been. The Reform Bill in fact served to preserve the predominance of the landed interest and of the aristocracy.[xviii] The next crucial step after the Reform Bill was the reform of the Poor Laws.

Poor Law Problems
With the spread of enclosures after 1760 and the rise in food prices during the French wars, the number of poor to be relieved increased rapidly, and the poor rates jumped accordingly. In 1775 they had amounted to less than £2 million, by 1801 they had doubled, and in 1831 they were nearly £7 million. In response, parishes attempted to supplement earnings with an allowance related to the prevailing price of bread. This came to be called the 'The Speenhamland System', which was developed by a meeting of Berkshire magistrates at Speen near Reading in 1795.[xix] It was adopted more widely after the end of the Napoleonic wars in 1815, but with variations from parish to parish; in Bicester, Oxfordshire,

it was called the 'roundsmen' system. It encouraged employers to reduce wages in the knowledge that the parish would make up the difference. A further consequence was a general depression of wages which threw even more people on to poor relief. In 1821, in Bicester, for example, there was a move to end the 'roundsmen' system, which the Poor Law Commissioner saw as a disaster 'because it destroys the connexion between work & wages'. By 1827 the system was not supported by a 'great part of the laboring population'. In 1831, Lord Chetwynd used his influence to end the system, both in Bicester and in the county generally i.e. farming the poor, with the Vestry paying for the employment and maintenance of the poor in the workhouse. In 1832, the year of the first cholera outbreak, outdoor relief in Bicester reached its height. One fifth of residents were declared paupers and expenditure on poor relief rose to £3,752 from £332 in 1776.[xx] Nationally these increases and the social unrest caused by them, convinced the government that reform was required, and this led to the Poor Law Amendment Act of 1834.

Under this Act, a new central board of commissioners was appointed, the old parish workhouses were abolished and the parishes grouped together in 'Unions', each with one large workhouse. Boards of Guardians were elected by the ratepayers in each Poor Law Union. Outdoor relief was abolished and conditions in the workhouse were made 'less eligible'. This meant that 'No relief would be given to an able bodied person outside of the workhouse', and 'Conditions in the workhouse should be less desirable than that of the lowest class of labourer to discourage the need to enter for relief and encourage the poor to support themselves.'[xxi] 'The New Poor Law was a blatant piece of class legislation, which trampled on the labouring poor, making the workhouse 'a terror and shame to ordinary people'. However, it also had a particular relevance to the story of emigration, as for the first time it encouraged the passage of poor families to America and the British colonies with the support of the new Poor Law Unions. This led to significant growth in emigration, and between 1835 and 1840 over 19,000 people were assisted by Poor Law Guardians in the agricultural counties of the South and the East. As noted above, prior to 1840, 983,227 left the UK, of whom the bulk went to North America, while 58,449 went to Australia and New Zealand.

The Chartists and the Repeal of the Corn Laws
The social unrest and violence noted above continued through most of the 1840s, supported by the Chartists, who published their People's Charter in May 1838. They were led by Feargus O'Connor, who became MP for Nottingham from 1847-52. They organised a number of riots and strikes, including the Birmingham Bull Ring Riots in July 1839, and the Newport rising in November 1839, which was

followed by mass arrests of Chartists. These included John Frost, Zephaniah Williams and William Jones, who were convicted and transported to Tasmania. In August 1842, strikes in the coalfields and other industries led to a general strike for the Chartists, and the Plug Riots, so called because the rioters attacked mills and drew the plugs from the boilers to stop the machinery, which brought the North to a standstill. As part of their programme, the Chartist Land Company bought five estates, including Charterville in Minster Lovell, near Witney in 1847. It was occupied in 1848, the peak year for the Chartists. In the same year, a Chartist 'Memorial of the inhabitants of Banbury' stated that 'a great portion of you Memorialists are now, and have long been, suffering unparalleled distress'. The number of emigrants from the town, and its immediate vicinity, was sufficient to justify a special 'Banbury Emigration Account' on which cheques were drawn to pay paupers' passage money. [xxii]

This social unrest put the government under great pressure to repeal the Corn Laws, which were first introduced as protective duties on corn in 1804. They were reintroduced in the Act of 1815 to protect the landed interest following the collapse of the artificially high prices caused by the Napoleonic Wars. The Act prohibited the import of corn and the price of bread, kept higher than it might have been, made post-war adjustment more difficult than necessary. The most sustained and politically effective criticism came from the Manchester-based Anti-Corn Law League from 1838 to 1846. They presented the Corn Laws as the epitome of the inefficiency and immorality of the old regime, and created a climate of opinion in favour of reform. It was Sir Robert Peel, as Prime Minister, who took the decision to repeal the Corn Laws in 1846. In doing so, he acted in defiance of the bedrock of the Tory Party, and thrust them into parliamentary opposition for the following thirty years. However, his decision also had a major effect on the future economy. 'In the decade from the mid-1840s to the mid-1850s, British imports and exports doubled, ushering in the mid-Victorian period's prosperity'. It also led to the Great Exodus of people emigrating to find a better way of life elsewhere, particularly in the United States (see Chapter 6). 'In the sixty years from American independence to 1845, only 1.6 million people entered the young republic, but in the following ten years 1.8 million would do so from Britain and Ireland alone.'[xxiii]

The next chapter charts the progress of emigration from Oxfordshire and the neighbouring shires from 1815 to 1850, including the effect of the Poor Law Amendment Act.

Chapter 4

Emigration from Oxfordshire and Neighbouring Buckinghamshire, Northamptonshire and Warwickshire, 1815-1850

a) Oxfordshire

It is important to remember that this project is dealing with the county of Oxfordshire long before its union with Berkshire in 1974. The notes below aim to provide a brief picture of the county as it was in the 19th century.[xxiv]

The County in the 19th Century

1. *The Topography*

The county has three predominant regions: the north-west is an area of uplands which extends approximately from Burford to Mollington, north of Banbury, with two broad blocks of higher land. The broad central plain lies to the south and east of Oxford, and the landscape is relatively flat and contains most of the county's floodlands. The third region is the Chiltern Hills, where the county contains part of the steep slope of this chalk range, and the change in topography is very apparent when viewed from the central plain.

2. *The Waterways*

The county's waterways reached a peak of national significance in 1790, with the completion of the Oxford Canal linking Banbury and Oxford with the Midlands. Of more consequence in the county was the establishment of local wharfs along the Oxford Canal, locations for coal merchants, kilns for bricks, lime and malt, and public houses, often kept by coal merchants or boat owners. For example, the Grantham family's wharf at Lower Heyford was Bicester's link to the waterways system, and for a time the inmates of its workhouse collected coal there. Several distinct canal communities grew up, in Banbury around the wharfs and boat-building yard in Mill Lane, and in Oxford in Fisher Row, where the old-established Beesley family became prominent canal boat men. Narrow boats continued the canal trade in the 20th century, with a boost in carrying during the Second World War.

Map of Oxfordshire and neighbouring shires (Julie Barrett).

3. *The Railways*

The railway reached Oxford in 1844, and within 20 years the railways had been extended to most other county towns, reaching Banbury (1850), Bicester (1850-1), Charlbury (1853), Chipping Norton (1855), Witney (1861) and Thame (1862). Bampton, Burford and Deddington did not have direct rail links and they had all lost their markets by the end of the 19th century. The railways also opened up markets for milk in London, Oxford, Reading and the Midlands, and Rider Haggard heard in the Cherwell Valley that 'the railroad [was] nicknamed the Milky Way'.

4. *Agriculture*

Arthur Young's survey in 1807 identified the county as an area of mixed farming, dominated by arable, with the Redlands in the north particularly praised for its rotations and its mix of wheat, barley, oats, and turnips with clover and beans. After 1815, post-war slump and fluctuating trade conditions slowed the pace of change. However, the third quarter of the 19th century, the era of Victorian High Farming, saw an improvement in fortunes with more modern production methods coinciding with relative lack of competition. This prosperity did not survive the mid-1870s, which saw the beginning of a prolonged agricultural depression. It also saw dairying became increasingly important to the county's agriculture (see Chapter 5 for more details). The Return of Owners of Land, 1873, revealed that Oxfordshire was the English county fourth least dominated by great estates (over 10,000 acres). Only the Duke of Marlborough at Blenheim fell into this category, with 21,000 acres. It was the 94 gentry estates (1,000-10,000 acres) which characterised the county. In these terms, Oxfordshire was the third most gentrified of all English counties (see Table 7 and Chapter 6).

5. *Industry*

The making of woollen textiles, slop clothing, gloves, lace and chairs employed several thousand people in the mid-19th century, many of them women. Textile manufacturers in the Banbury area specialized in the production of plush by the 1790s. Plush was used for upholstery, hats and liveries, and for finishing processes in the manufacture of other high quality fabrics. It remained a rural and domestic industry, with weavers in Shutford, Bloxham, Adderbury and Banbury. By 1851 it was more concentrated in Banbury, where there were 123 weavers and 16 ancillary workers. By 1871, there were only 52 weavers in Banbury but William Wrench was still employing 28 at Shutford.

In Chipping Norton there were four textile manufacturers in the 1790s, all of them taking in cloth from domestic weavers. By 1851, the descendants of one of them, Thomas Bliss, had built a mill for making woollen cloth, managed by a Yorkshireman. In 1872, it was replaced by one of Oxfordshire's most spectacular industrial buildings. By 1891, William Bliss was employing 581 people, most working in the factory and living in Chipping Norton. They included many migrants from other textile regions.

Witney blanket manufacture moved from the rural workshops to factory based organization by the 1850s. The trade flourished with the introduction of mechanized spinning and carding, spring looms and, from the 1850s, power looms. In the 1860s, the industry employed over 600 people and production was concentrated in Witney, where manufacturers continued to build new mills into the 20th century.

Woodstock was celebrated for glove making before 1700 and the trade expanded during the Napoleonic Wars. By 1839, about 150 men and around 1,000 women were employed. In 1871, there were 133 glove-makers in Woodstock itself, and 88 in Old Woodstock, and there were six glove manufacturers. Glove making was also extensive in the parishes to the north and east and it was almost as important in Witney and its townships. William Prichett of Newland, Witney, employed over 500 people.

Chair making in the Chilterns centred on High Wycombe, but extended into Oxfordshire, and many chair turners made components e.g. 57 in Chinnor. Pillow lace was manufactured across a large area of Buckinghamshire, Bedfordshire and Northamptonshire, and on the eastern fringes of Oxfordshire. Factors distributed work to, and collected finished products from, women working mostly at home. Bicester had 77 lacemakers in 1861. The density in other parishes varied considerably, with 53 in Souldern, 52 in Stoke Lyne and 35 in Mixbury, all in the Cherwell Valley, but in many villages there were very few or none. After 1870, lace making became industrialized and hand-made lace declined as a source of income for poorer families.

6. *Brewing and Malting*

The mid-19th century was the high point for both brewing and malting. The 18th century had seen the emergence of the great brewing families the Halls, Treachers, Morrells and Tawneys, but there were also numerous small concerns and publican brewers. A good local example of the industrial Victorian brewery was Hunt Edmunds of Banbury, started by Thomas and John Hunt of the Unicorn Inn. Their development was completed in 1866 with a great new malthouse. Others replaced old premises with a new type of building the tower brewery; Phillips in Oxford, and the Hook Norton Brewery built such towers. By 1860 every town had at least one brewery, and some had many more e.g. 14 in Oxford, ten in Banbury and seven in Bicester, making a total of 70. By 1910 these had dwindled to 18. This reflects a national trend – of 50,000 breweries in the UK in 1840 barely 3,000 were left by 1900.

Population Changes

Table 2 shows the growth in the population of Oxfordshire between 1801 and 1851: 124% urban growth (Oxford and Banbury) and 39% rural growth (including small towns). Between 1851 and 1901, the Table shows urban growth of 72% but a 6% decline in the rural population. Table 3 shows that the peak population of most of the selected villages was between 1851 and 1871, prior to the agricultural depressions. Fritwell was a notable exception in attaining its peak in 1891 but it was well known for its expert craftsmen and tradesmen and also for its Methodism.

Table 2
Population Growth in Oxfordshire, 1801-1911

	1801	1851	Growth %	1911	Growth %
Oxfordshire	111,977	170,434	52.2	189,484	11
Oxford,inc. Suburbs	13,421	30,410	122.8	52,979	74
Banbury inc.Suburbs	3,810	8,206	115.4	13,458	64
Urban Oxfordshire (Oxford + Banbury)	17,231	38,616	124.1	66,437	72
Rural Oxfordshire (inc. Small towns*)	94,746	131,818	39.1	123,047	-6

* The small towns were Bampton, Bicester, Burford, Charlbury, Chipping Norton, Deddington, Eynsham, Henley-on-Thames, Thame, Watlington, and Woodstock.

Individual Parishes

The Oxfordshire records examined show that the following parishes, with the support of the local Vestries (representatives of local ratepayers who dealt with parochial business) and their respective Poor Law Unions, both encouraged and assisted emigration.[xxv] No doubt there were many other parishes which had the same experience.

Table 3
Population in Oxfordshire, 1801-1911

Village	1801	1851	1871	1891	1911	Decline % (Note 2)
Banbury Poor Law Union						
Bloxham (Note 3)	1,157	1,336	1,477	1,340	1,335	13%
Hornton (Note 3)	485	591	561	426	379	35%
Sibfords	610	**899**	757	696	633	33%
Tadmarton	387	**450**	434	320	318	33%
Bicester Poor Law Union						
Fringford	252	357	**479**	403	374	21%
Fritwell	396	514	552	**560**	453	19%
Launton	372	706	**746**	619	544	27%
Brackley Poor Law Union						
Finmere	308	**399**	327	283	222	44%
Chipping Norton Poor Law Union						
Leafield	487	837	**896**	734	671	25%
Milton-under-Wychwood	495	799	**962**	898	707	26%
Shipton-under-Wychwood	406	616	**761**	743	654	14%
Headington Poor Law Union						
Cuddesdon	244	337	**410**	343	274	33%
Thame Poor Law Union						
Great Milton	509	**643**	618	547	439	31%
Wallingford Poor Law Union						
Dorchester (Note 3)	777	872	866	852	804	11%
Witney Poor Law Union						
South Leigh	240	**359**	320	325	293	18%
Woodstock Poor Law Union						
Deddington	1,552	**2,178**	2,061	1,777	1,456	33%
Tackley (Note 3)	368	558	570	506	451	19%
Wootton	823	**1,250**	1,231	1,069	610*	39%
Town						Growth % 1851-1911
Banbury	3,810	8,206	9,863	9,792	**13,458**	64%
Bicester	1,946	3,054	3,328	3,343	**3,385**	10%
Chipping Norton	1,812	2,932	3,641	**4,222**	3,972	35%
Oxford	13,421	27,843	31,404	45,742	**52,979**	90%
* new boundaries						
Oxfordshire	111,977	170,434	177,960	185,274	**189,484**	11%
UK	15.7m	27.3m	31.4m	37.8m	**42m**	53%

Notes
1. **Bold type** = peak population, 1801-1911.
2. Decline % from peak population.
3. Other peak dates

1841 Hornton 592	1881 Bloxham 1,538	
1861 Dorchester 925; Tackley 626		

Banbury Poor Law Union

Adderbury

29 May 1845. The following embarked on the *Royal Albert* to Canada: John Adams, 39, Mary, 34, William, 15; George West, 28, Caroline, 29, and 3 children; Joseph Parker, 24, Elisabeth, 25; William West, 40, Mary Ann, 38, and 6 children.

April 1848, The Poor Law records show that several pauper families emigrated to Australia. The parish at that time was suffering particularly from a decline in the local plush industry.[xxvi]

Banbury

In April 1847, the *Banbury Guardian* commented that 'a considerable number of persons are this season emigrating from this neighbourhood to the United States and Canada'.

Milton, Adderbury East

4 May 1847, To Canada: William Taylor, 38, Susannah, 38, and 6 children.

Bloxham

2 March 1836, to Upper Canada: Thomas Taylor, 28, Elizabeth, 30, and 5 children. Two other unnamed families emigrated by privately raised funds.

Bodicote

24 March 1849, To Australia: Thomas Boffin, 54, widower, David, 26, Susanna, 25, William, 19, single; Thomas Wiggins, Edward Perry (?), 18, Charles Shuckle (?), 20, mason; Charles Claridge, 20, mason; Henry Chilton, 17.

Chacombe

April 1848, The Poor Law records show that several families emigrated to Australia. The parish raised £16 to defray the expenses of its pauper emigrants. They may have been framework knitters, who were declining in numbers in the village at this period.[xxvii]

Hook Norton

15 May/3 June?1849, To Canada on the *Victoria*: Richard Eden, 28, Sarah, 28, and 6 children; Jesse Hopkins, 44, Louisa, 42, and 6 children; George Phipps, 40, Mary, 35, and 5 children; Thomas Miller, 48, Dorcas, 46, and 4 children.

South Newington

The population peaked at 462 in 1831, and then declined to 222 in 1911. Much of the decline in the 1840s and 1850s was ascribed to emigration, which was encouraged and partly financed by the parish authorities.

17 May 1845, the following embarked on the *Saint Anne* to Canada: Jonas Page, 30, Esther, 25, William, 4, Frederick 1, Luke, 18 (a cousin); Joseph Beck, 35, Harriet, 31, Fanny, 8, Richard, 1; John Page, 31, Mary, 29, 2 children, Anne, 23, single; William Cordner, 24; William Parsons, 18; Henry Baron (?), 22; John Hartly, 21; Chris Nelson (?), 18; George Hions, 24; William Waite, 18; William Dale, 30.

Tadmarton
1 June 1849, To Australia: Henry Hopkins, 19/20, single, Ann, 58/60, widow, Hannah, 17, single, full account of expenses, 4 May 1850.

Bicester Poor Law Union
Bicester
In 1830, a free emigration system to the United States was organized by the Bicester Emigration Committee. This happened very quickly after a similar meeting in King's Sutton (see below).

24 May 1830, 71 adults and 40 children were conveyed by wagons to Liverpool with the expectation of getting a passage to America. The party seems to have reached Liverpool on 27 May in just 5 days compared with 8 days for the King's Sutton group. £1000 was borrowed from the rates to finance the scheme. There are details of the expenditure involved and of communications with Mr George of Bicester, and of Samuel Foster and William Paxton, who had travelled ahead of the party to arrange shipping.. They contracted with Samuel McPherson for the passages of from 70 to 100 Persons to sail on Monday (31 May) if the wind is fair. Leyland & Bullens (Bank) are prepared to pay the £800 and have furnished us with cheques to draw upon them. The ship engaged was the *Warren*, commanded by Capt Carr.[xxviii] In the event six members of two Blencowe families did not join the party, so the total was reduced to 105. It seems that they lost heart and worked their way back to Bicester, where they were set to work fetching coal in a barrow from the Lower Heyford wharf. But it was resolved that they do apply to the Overseers for an alteration of employment.[xxix]

Chesterton
27 April 1844, 9 Kings and 4 Beaseleys left the parish to embark on the *Templar* on May 1st from Deptford to Sydney.

2 August 1845, Two villagers perished in the *Cataraqui* disaster (see Tackley below and Appendix 1.

Fringford
2 August 1845. Seven villagers perished in the *Cataraqui* disaster (see Tackley below and Appendix 1).

Fritwell
2 August 1845, Two villagers perished in the *Cataraqui* disater (see Tackley below and Appendix 1).

Lower Heyford
April 1848, about 15 persons left Lower Heyford to emigrate to America, in the splendid ship called the *'New World'*.

Stoke Lyne
10 May 1845, Richard Buswell and 6 family members to Quebec.
    2 August 1845, Five villagers perished in the *Cataraqui* disaster (see Tackley below and Appendix 1).

Brackley (Northants) Poor Law Union
Finmere
In 1831, money from the rates was paid to help families to emigrate. The Paxton family (one of the leading farmers) was the first to go. In 1832, four more families left for New York

Headington Poor Law Union
Cuddesdon
In 1832, overseers tried to encourage emigration by distributing pamphlets, and in 1839, £60 was raised to help the poor to emigrate.

Stanton St John
17 Feb 1840, £40 borrowed from the Trustees for purposes of emigration plus 8 shillings, one year's interest.

Henley Poor Law Union
Pyrton
About 1848, some labourers emigrated at the expense of the parish, but it was said that others were undesirables and were rejected by the Emigration Commissioners.

Thame Poor Law Union
Great Haseley
2 August 1845. Seven villagers perished in the *Cataraqui* disaster (see Tackley below and Appendix 1.

Thame

There were serious problems with poverty and unemployment in the 1830s and 1840s. They reached a critical stage in 1847-48, when there were 398 inmates in the new workhouse - 400 being the official limit. Local parishes were empowered to establish Emigration Funds, and Thame were sanctioned to raise £50.

Aston Rowant and (Bucks) Bledlow

In 1843, 'One hundred and thirty emigrants left Aylesbury railway station this morning: they are going out to Port Philip {Melbourne}: they were mostly from Chinnor and neighbourhood.' The party leaving Liverpool on 3 November 1843 included James Croxford, 26, ag.lab, Presbyterian, from Aston Rowant, and Elizabeth (27), with sons Francis, 5, and Reuben, 3. They arrived in Port Philip, NSW, on 16 February 1844, after 106 days, with 307 passengers.

In 1848, Eden White, 18, shepherd, Richard White, 20, and Emma Smith, 22, dairy maid, boarded the *Mahomed Shah*, sailing from London and Plymouth on 29 March 1848, arriving in Port Philip on 5 July 1848, with 211 emigrants on board.

In 1850, Jonah Britnell, 18, baker at Bledlow with his wife Sarah, domestic servant of the Vicarage, Bledlow, boarded the *Statesman* sailing from London and Plymouth, arriving in Port Philip on 17 March 1850. Their 6 children were all born in Victoria.[xxx]

Wallingford (Berks) Poor Law Union

Dorchester

In the 1820s, emigration became a popular way of helping the poor. In 1829, the overseers spent £29 17s in sending 2 men to America, the passage costing £17. In 1832, a family of 7 emigrated at a cost to the parish of £30.

Witney Poor Law Union

Bampton

From the 1820s, poverty and unemployment prompted large scale emigration to America and the British colonies. This was actively promoted by the Vestry, and continued in the 1850s. Ad hoc committees were increasingly appointed to oversee poor relief, and to allocate clothing and tools for emigrants.

Eynsham

By 1832, the Vestry complained of payments to the unemployed of about £350, and recommended funding emigration.

Witney
In the 1840s, there was a 9% fall in population because of blanket industry problems and early mechanization. Emigration to Australia, the Cape of Good Hope, and America is mentioned throughout the period.

Woodstock Poor Law Union
Begbroke
In 1823, Michael Steel (at his own expense) emigrated from Begbroke to Van Diemen's Land (VDL) with his sister, Jane, and two servants. They sailed on the *Mariner* on 17 May, carrying merchandise and 57 passengers, and arrived in Hobart on 26 September (see Chapter 8).

Deddington
In 1831, 50 were sent to North America, but the death of most of them from cholera on board temporarily 'damped the spirit of emigration in the district'. In 1836-47, despite the the opposition of the incumbent, the Revd William Risley, over £230 was raised for emigration.

Kiddington
2 August 1845, seven villagers perished in the *Cataraqui* disaster (see Tackley below and Appendix 1).

Rousham
2 August 1845, Emily Walton (18) perished in the *Cataraqui* disaster (see Tackley below and Appendix 1).

Steeple Barton
In 1846, emigration to the USA, Canada and Australia was encouraged and assisted.

Stonesfield
In 1841-51, the population dropped slightly, partly due to emigration of poor families, encouraged and assisted by Vestry. In 1845, 15 villagers drowned on the *Cataraqui* going to Port Phillip (Melbourne) (see also Tackley and Appendix 1). In 1861, the population peaked at 650, but emigration largely balanced a natural increase from migration (probably for quarrying).

Tackley
The Cataraqui Disaster
On 3 February 1845, the Tackley Vestry met and resolved to encourage the following 42 to emigrate: William Cook, 39, Anne and 6 children; John Ryman,

29, Hannah and 3 children; Antony Merry, 37, Edith, and 9 children; Robert Hoare, 26, Emma, 23, and 3 children; James Cook, 27, Anne, 23, and 3 children. All the men were agricultural labourers.

This move may have been in response to an advertisement on the front page of *Jackson's Oxford Journal* for 18 January 1845. This ad offered Free Passage to Australia, to sail on 1st March to Port Phillip [Melbourne], and the description of the ship fits the *Cataraqui*. The Vestry also agreed to borrow £150 to defray the expense of emigration. Somehow they managed to repay this debt in only ten weeks, although repayment was planned over five years. It seems probable that the hand of a benefactor, or a group, must have been responsible.

The emigrants left Tackley on 13 April 1845 in company with others from Kiddington (9), Rousham (1), Stoke Lyne (5), Stonesfield (15), and Wootton (4), and were conducted to Liverpool. They boarded the *Cataraqui*, as did more local people from Chesterton (2), Fringford (7), Fritwell (4), and Great Haseley (7) (see Appendix 1). The ship was an 800 ton barque, built in Canada in 1840 and named after a tributary of the St Lawrence River. She was classified A1 by Lloyds. She sailed on 20 April for Port Phillip.

The disastrous wreck occurred on 4 August 1845 off the uninhabited King Island in the Bass Straits between Tasmania and Australia, just one day short of their destination. The ship sunk and broke up, leaving 399 dead and only 9 survivors (8 of them crewmen). They were eventually picked up and delivered to Melbourne on 13 September (see Chapter 7).[xxxi]

Woodstock
In 1834-5, Vestry agreed to pay for two families to emigrate to America. James Hedges, possibly at the Glove House workshop by 1820, was one of those convicted and demonstrated against for 'trucking'. Under this practice, certain workers, particularly navvies, were paid partly in goods and partly in tokens exchangeable only at shops owned by the employers. The Truck Act 1831 aimed to curtail this practice. Hedges emigrated in 1833.

Wootton
After 1835, when Wootton became part of the Woodstock Union, Vestry initiated provision of cheap coal to the poor and collection of a small fund to encourage emigration. Four people from Wootton perished in the *Cataraqui* disaster in 1845 (see Tackley above and Appendix 1).

B. Buckinghamshire

The County in the 19th Century

1. *The Topography*

The County is divided into two sections, to the south from the Thames up to the Chiltern Hills and to the north the Vale of Aylesbury. After 1850 the expansion of the railways helped the development of towns like Aylesbury, Amersham and High Wycombe but bypassed Buckingham and Olney, leaving them less populous. The Return of Owners of Land in 1873 revealed very similar results to Oxfordshire, with two great estates (over 10,000 acres) belonging to Lord Carington and Earl Brownlow of Berkhamsted, and a further 81 estates over 1,000 acres. The 22 estates over 3,000 acres included the Duke of Buckingham at Stowe with 9,511 acres, Baron L.N. de Rothschild with 9,959 acres at Waddesdon, and Sir Henry Verney of Claydon House with 6,688 acres; also Lord Overstone with 5,072 acres, who also owned land in Northamptonshire and Warwickshire. There were also 71 estates over 1,000 acres (see Table 7 and Chapter 6).

2. *Rivers and Canals*

The county has two major rivers, the Thames on its south-west border and the Great Ouse, which rises in Northamptonshire just out of the county but flows east through Buckingham. The main branch of the Grand Union Canal passes through the county.

3. *Agriculture*

Agriculture predominated and there was little heavy industry and quarrying. There was an increase in pastoral farming with smaller area of crops, so labour needs declined. Sheep provided meat for the growing London market and their wool was a by-product. The years 1851-75 were good for farming and the county's home market was protected from competition by foreign wars e.g. the Crimean and French Wars. The development of the railways, with a reduction in transport costs, meant that urban demand for milk, butter, cheese and eggs could be exploited. Milk production was favoured and between 1895 and 1914 milk consumption doubled. At the same time, the farming depression led many to move to Wolverton and Bletchley to railway companies.

4. *Other Sources of Income*

Straw plaiting and lace making, which had made contributions to many poorer families, were both in decline after 1870. Machinery destroyed hand-lace making, which had flourished in the South Midlands. At the same time,

Table 4
Population in Buckinghamshire, 1801-1911

Village	1801	1851	1871	1891	1911	Decline % (Note 2)
Aylesbury Poor Law Union						
Grendon Underwood (Note 3)	285	427	448	373	303	32%
Oving	257	**442**	440	364	318	28%
Quainton (Note 3)	870	945	921	885	895	17%
Buckingham Poor Law Union						
Maids Moreton	239	**573**	511	444	371	35%
Marsh Gibbon	534	**944**	876	696	587	37%
Padbury (Note 3)	459	660	601	490	442	37%
Preston Bissett	322	**554**	485	311	285	48%
Stowe	311	**342**	370	311	251	26%
Thornborough (Note 3)	458	754	687	564	443	41%
Tingewick	642	877	**945**	**714**	663	29%
(Oxon) Thame Poor Law Union						
Brill (Note 3)	859	1,311	1,363	1,251	1,121	22%
Long Crendon	991	**1,700**	1,365	1,187	1,082	36%
Winslow Poor Law Union						
East Claydon (Note 3)	299	361	376	343	280	27%
Great Horwood	537	834	**866**	639	584	32%
Swanbourne (Note 3)	529	646	558	429	427	37%
Town						Growth% 1851-1911
Aylesbury	3,186	6,081	6,962	8,680	**11,048**	81%
Bletchley	824	1,303	1,619	3,070	**5,166**	296%
Buckingham (Note 3)	2,605	4,020	3,703	3,364	3,282	(-18%)
High Wycombe	4,248	7,179	10,492	16,409	**20,337**	183%
Buckinghamshire	107,900	163,723	175,926	185,458	**219,551**	34%

Notes
1. **Bold type** = peak population 1801-1911
2. Decline % from peak population.
3. Other peak dates

1831	Padbury	708	1841 Quainton	1,081
1831	Buckingham	4,054	Swanbourne	679
1831	Brill	1,449	1861 East Claydon	385
1841	Thornborough	762	1861 Grendon Underwood	451

education for children aged 10 was made compulsory, so that they could no longer make any money for their families.

Population Changes

Table 4 shows the significant increases in the population of a sample of Buckinghamshire villages from 1801 to 1851, most of them achieving their peak by 1851. However, it also shows that by 1911 all the village populations had declined significantly by from 22% to 48%. In the same period, the populations of the towns had increased dramatically except for Buckingham's which had declined by 18%. The sample of villages is mostly taken from ones bordering Oxfordshire.

Emigration

General Information
Buckinghamshire Poor Law Unions
2 July 1844, Certificate through Messrs Carter & Bonus from Chief Emigrant officer at Quebec for conveyance of 25.

Individual Parishes

Buckingham Poor Law Union
Tingewick
In 1832, John and Frances Cross emigrated to Van Diemens Land on the *Forth*. arriving at the VDL's Land Company's settlement at Stanley, Circular Head, on 6 April 1832. The Revd William Palmer, Rector of Finmere, had assisted them in the emigration process. Finding unsatisfactory conditions inconsistent with the terms of their hire, they and others left and got to Launceston where they settled. John died after working in the building industry in 1840. Frances died in 1852.[xxxii]

Twyford
14 July 1848, Sophia Wise (née Thorpe) and her husband, William, with their two surviving children, emigrated to Australia on the *Emperor* from Plymouth, arriving at Sydney on 4 November 1848. William already had a brother, Joseph, in the colony, who had arrived at Port Philip on the *Palmyra* in July 1848. William and Sophia first settled in the Bathurst area, which was opened up after the crossing of the Blue Mountains. They remained in Bathurst until 1860 when they bought property in the Milthorpe area. Sophia died in 1896 and William in 1900, both being buried at Milthorpe.[xxxiii]

Newport Pagnell Poor Law Union
Great Linford
15 Feb 1844, Memo of Great Linford Parish meeting on assisted emigration with names and calculations. It was considered that about £200 must be raised for such a purpose and it was decided that a 4 penny rate should be raised amongst the occupiers of land which would amount to about £40 plus such a rate upon the land owners would amount to about £160 - £200. Names given and ages (some deleted, so a confused picture): Rileys and 7 children, and Fennels and 6 children. Mr Marsh would be ready to go with him (possibly with Mr Goss, wife and 5 children) on 1st April provided he had £20. See Chapter 7 for costs involved.[xxxiv]

Woughton
1 Dec 1848, Letter from Thomas Drew to Frederick Druce (from Great Brickhill to Woughton). 'Helping Mr Nicholls to emigrate provided he is entirely guided by Mr Levi. He applied to me yesterday for an order for the Workhouse- in order not to disqualify him. I have given him 3 loaves till I know Mr Levi's mind on the matter. He wants to send the money by this night's post.'[xxxv]
9 Dec 1848, Notice of Meeting to consent to raising or borrowing Money for Emigration Purposes; also printed forms as completed for the item above.[xxxvi]

C. Northamptonshire

The County in the 19th Century

1. *The Topography*
The county is divided into two distinct areas: the highland north and east with heavy clay soils, and the lowlands to the south with light and medium loams. Mention should also be made of the forest regions of Rockingham, Salsey and Whittlewood, and the Soke of Peterborough with a large area of high heath and extended marsh in the Borough Great Fen. In 1823, the county 'was said to {enjoy} a very pure and wholesome air because of its dryness and distance from the sea.' Towns were of small importance except for Northampton and Peterborough. In summer it hosted a great number of wealthy families and it was called the county of 'spires and squires' i.e. ancient churches and stately homes. This was confirmed by the results of the Return of Owners of Land in 1873 which revealed that the county had more great estates over 10,000 acres (5) and more gentry with over 3,000 acres (28) than the other three shires which were also well gentrified (see Table 7 and Chapter 6). The great estates included the Duke of Buccleuch with 17,965 acres, the Marquis of Exeter of Burghley, Stamford, with 13,545, the Hon George W. Fitzwilliam with 18,116, Lord Overstone with 15,045 and Earl Spencer with 17,080.

Table 5
Population in Northamptonshire, 1801-1911

Village	1801	1851	1871	1891	1911	Decline% (Note 2)
Brackley Poor Law Union						
Chipping Warden (Note 3)	294	521	480	345	347	33%
Eydon (Note 3)	484	621	531	397	431	30%
Evenley	369	489	**589**	451	363	38%
Helmdon	421	603	**656**	502	439	27%
King's Sutton	1,021	**1,335**	1,319	1,139	1,181	11%
Syresham	587	**1,027**	991	773	654	34%
Daventry Poor Law Union						
Braunston (Note 3)	909	**1,253**	1,070	983	1,059	28%
Everdon (Note 3)	588	712	672	497	476	38%
Preston Capes (Note 3)	380	363	283	205	193	56%
Kettering Poor Law Union						
Pytchley (Note 3)	361	606	547	525	535	17%
Towcester Poor Law Union						
Blisworth (Note 3)	730	951	978	930	823	13%
Greens Norton	615	887	**892**	829	791	18%
Silverstone	586	1,134	**1,163**	1,125	981	15%
Weedon Lois	387	**545**	538	397	354	34%
						Growth %
Town						1851-1911
Brackley	1,495	2,297	2,331	2,614	**2,633**	14%
Daventry	2,562	**4,430**	4,051	3,939	3,516	(-20%)
Towcester	2,030	2,665	2,677	**2,775**	2,340	(-12%)
Northampton	7,027	26,657	41,168	61,016	**90,064**	237%
Wellingborough	3,325	5,297	9,355	15,068	**19,753**	272%
					1,901	
Northamptonshire	131,757	212,380	268,891	302,150	**338,051**	59%

Notes

1. **Bold type** = peak population 1801-1911
2. Decline % from peak population.
3. Other peak dates

1821	Pytchley	652	1841	Everdon		777
	Preston Capes	441		Eydon		647
	Braunston	1,469	1861	Blisworth		1,022
	Chipping Warden	539				

2. *Rivers and Canals*
The county contains the watershed between the Severn and the Wash. Several rivers have their sources in the north west of the county, including the Nene, which flows north-east to the Wash, and the Warwickshire Avon, which flows south-west to the Severn. The Oxford and Grand Union Canals join the county at Braunston. The Blisworth Tunnel, which was finally completed in 1805, at 2,813 metres is the third longest in the United Kingdom. Stoke Bruerne has the famous Canal Museum.

3. *Agriculture*
By 1850, the county was still predominantly dependent on agriculture. There seems to have been little unrest compared to other counties, indicating that lands were improved and that agriculture remained profitable to farmers. The north and east were predominantly arable, while the south and west were pasture, although there was a shift to arable in the period 1850-70, and a move to dairying later.

4. *Industry*
a. *Shoemaking and Leather Working*
The county is best known for its shoemaking and leather working and in 1914 it was said that half the county's population worked in them. Access to raw materials was guaranteed by the large cattle market. The central location enabled a wide distribution, so that shoemaking became Northampton's major industry. In 1841, there were 1,821 shoemakers in the town – some were described as manufacturers who employed a large number of shoemakers; they collected raw materials and returned the finished products to the manu-facturers. In 1857-8, there was widespread fear of mechanization and mass unemployment. However the threat of a strike came to nothing, as the shoemakers realised that they would benefit from mechanization. In 1858, Machine Sewn Tops were approved. In 1859, Isaac, Campbell & Co's factory was completed in Campbell Square. The company failed but in 1861 Turner Brothers took over and four years later they were producing 100,000 pairs of shoes per week. The business had moved from the workshop to the factory, as it did in other industries, but trade hand techniques lingered on into the 20th century. In the First World War, Northampton provided 23 million pairs of boots and shoes and the rest of the county another 24 million pairs.

b. *Ironstone Quarrying*
There was considerable ironstone quarrying in the north-west of the county from 1850, around Burton Latimer and Finedon. This was exploiting an ironstone bed

which runs from the vicinity of Lincoln in the north to Towcester in the south. The area gained considerable publicity in the Great Exhibition of 1851, where samples of ironstone from the estate of Colonel Arbuthnot of Woodford House were displayed, leading to the mass exploitation of the county's ironstone. It was also helped in 1857 by the opening of the railway mainline through Kettering en route from Leicester to Hitchin, and a branch railway from Kettering to Hitchin in 1866. These provided the impetus for quarrying ironstone on a grand scale as it could now be transported to centres for iron production. In 1866, Finedon had furnaces producing pig iron and in 1867 Thomas Butlin, a well known ironmaster, opened blast furnaces in Wellingborough. They also used furnaces in Derbyshire. Ironstone quarrying continued in the area for about a hundred years.

c. *Other Sources of Income*
Straw plaiting and lace making were other sources of income for poorer families for a long time. However, by the 1870s they were both in decline as they became industrialized. At the same time, school for children aged 10 became compulsory, so that they were not able to make any money.

Population Changes
Table 5 shows the significant growth in the population of a sample of Northamptonshire villages from 1801 to 1851, although some did not achieve their peak until 1871. By 1911, all the village populations had declined significantly by from 11% to 38%. In the same period, the populations of Northampton and Wellingborough increased significantly, while Brackley only grew by 14% and Daventry and Towcester both declined. The county's population also grew significantly. The sample of villages is mostly taken from ones bordering Oxfordshire.

Emigration

General Instructions
a. *9 June 1836, Circular from Colonial Emigration Agency Office to the Overseers of the parish of Warkworth, in the Hundred of King's Sutton:*
1. Most favorable season for emigrating to the United States and British America.
2. Advantages offered by this Office to Parish Authorities and Private Individuals re selection of appropriate vessels, and laying in provisions at lowest rates.
3. Many instances in past years of severe suffering and melancholy loss of life, improper selection of vessels and want of attention to quality and quantity of stores.

4. Inferior ships, emigrants find too late they have been induced to embark by interested parties with false plea of some trivial reduction to buy provisions in their shops at extravagant price.

5. (We) guarantee none but first class vessels and superior provisions & every human means are exercised to ensure the Emigrants safe and comfortable passages.[xxxvii]

b. *16 Aug 1839, Colonization Commissioners for South Australia, Regulations for Labourers wishing to emigrate to South Australia, which include the following:*

1. All must be married and aged between 15 and 30. Wives and children under 16 free. All must be vaccinated.

2. Emigrants must pay the expense of reaching the port of embarkation. Every emigrant may take half a ton weight, or twenty measured cubic feet of luggage.

3. Emigrants must provide the bedding for themselves and children and the necessary tools for their own trades.

4. On arrival they will be received by an Officer who will supply their immediate wants, and at all times give them employment *at reduced wages* on the Government works, if from any cause they should be unable to obtain it elsewhere. The Commissioners cannot give any exact information as to the amount of wages to be obtained, they can merely state that hitherto wages have been very much higher than in England.

c. *12 November 1839, Letter from South Australia Colonization Office, Adelphi Terrace, London to the Revd A.B.Brown of Pytchley:*

Considerable number of emigrants required for the *Morley* to sail on 2nd December and the *Eliza* on the 12th. You will oblige me by making public this intelligence amongst the Shepherds and Agricultural Labourers…and inform me what number of Married Couples you think might be depended on for these ships.'

d. *c.1840, Letter from the Foreign Office, No 17, Water Street, & 8, Redcross Street, Liverpool, signed by Galindo & Newman, Merchants..*

TO THE OVERSEERS OF THE PARISH OF

Gentlemen,

We forward the accompanying handbill, and submit to your consideration the fact that it would be far more economical (particularly in Manufacturing and Farming districts) to follow the example of many other parishes, and afford means of Emigration to the surplus and unemployed Population; thus at once relieving the Parish from the heavy burden of the Poor Rates.

Any number of persons above ten may be Shipped at a very small Charge when compared with the Rates: our Agent is empowered to enter into contract for their Passage, and will afford every information.

Gallindo & Newman,
Merchants

Respectable Persons and Families may also secure Cabin or Steerage Passages by the Packets to America or any other part of the world on application, postpaid, to our Agent for your district, as on the other side.

TO MECHANICS AND LABOURERS

The extensive Improvements now making throughout America afford to the above Classes of Persons an excellent opportunity of providing comfort for themselves and Families.

   The Railways, Canals, and increasing Manufactories now in progress in New York, Philadelphia, Baltimore, Boston, South Carolina, Virginia, Pennsylvania, &c, are sufficient to give employment for many years to ONE HUNDRED THOUSAND MEN. By the last advices Labourers are paid Sixteen Dollars per Month, and found their Provisions.

   Persons may book themselves, and receive Information by applying to Mr T.Freeman, Printer, Bookseller & Auctioneer, Market Square, Agent for Northampton.

   Of whom also Cabin Passages may be secured to all parts of the World. Respectable Applications for Agencies in any town (post paid) will be attended to.

e. *13 December 1845 Letter from Thomas Bosworth to his wife, Matilda,* includes the following:
'Mr and Mrs Richard Hayne from New Brunswick are there with six young ones - now young women. Mr Hayne wants some farmers to return with him in the Spring. Don't you think some of our young 'Labrin (sic) Jobs' could be spared.'

Individual Parishes
Banbury (Oxon) Poor Law Union
Chacombe
21April 1848, to Australia: William Bloxham, 34, Johannah, 29, lacemaker, and 3 children; John Gray, 33, Charlotte, 32, and 4 children.

Brackley Poor Law Union

Eydon

In 1835, the Poor Law Act gave parish overseers authority to borrow up to £100, to be deposited with the treasurer of the local union, to assist men to emigrate. Not more than 3d a mile to take emigrants to the port of emigration, £1 could be spent on clothing, 10s on bedding and utensils for each adult to fit them out for the journey. This scale applied 'For eastwards of the Cape of Good Hope'; higher for Australia. Eydon borrowed £75 from Gillett & Tawney, the Banbury bankers, giving an IOU signed by 13 parishioners.

26 March 1845, 4 men and 4 women, 8 children under 7, and 7 aged 7-14, left for Canada on the *Canton*.

10 May 1845, £62.10s. borrowed to enable Ann Willoughby, 48, with 7 children aged from 3-18, to emigrate on the *William Braham* and join her husband in Canada. There was delay and problems in repaying the debt.

But on 23 March 1850, the Vestry agreed that 2½d in the £ was to be collected, in total £26.17.2¾. They also agreed to a subscription of 5 farthings in the £ be collected, all to assist Isaac and George Jeffs and their families to emigrate to North America.[xxxviii]

Greatworth with Westthorp

1830 A group from Westhorp sailed to New York.

1836 A group of 3 families and 2 single men emigrated to America. Marston parish paid their passages, and gave each adult one sovereign and each child a ½ sovereign. The Guardians of the Poor of Marston had been authorized to raise £18 out of the Poor Rates for defraying the expenses of emigrants. Different amounts were payable for those going to the tropics or east of the Cape of Good Hope.

King's Sutton

In 1830, a party of 9 men, 5 women and 22 children emigrated from Liverpool to New York. They included the following: Wm Billington and 6 children, and the following with family: Thos Parish, Wm Jerome, Jas Taylor, and Jno Wilkings and the following alone: Edward Humfris, and Wm Parish. The records also include details of the cost of provisions for a man, wife and 6 children, and of the provisions purchased (see Chapter 7).[xxxix]

Kettering Poor Law Union

Broughton

On 6 December 1850, the Poor Law Board of Kettering authorized the Parish of Broughton to raise £48 for 'defraying the expenses of the Emigration of poor persons having settlement in the said Parish'.[xl]

Pytchley

18 Aug 1838, Letter from Rev'd A.W.Brown re Application for Free Passage to South Australia of the following: Joseph Flavel, agricultural labourer, 40, Mary, 39, with 7 children and infant born 10 days ago; James and Mary Dainty, and 4 children. Passage for 9 children to be paid by a parish officer (9x £3 = £27), all necessary comforts provided before they go on board, expenses to London and other expenses (List given in Chapter 7).[xli]

12 March 1844, Expenses of the Faulkners and party from Pytchley to Melbourne: Abraham Faulkner, wife and 5 children; John Shearhog, wife Alice Waring, John Waring, young man, who all left Pytchley on 12 March to embark in London (See Chapter 7 for further details).[xlii]

28 January 1846, Letter to the Rev'd A.W.Brown of Pytchley from Colonial and Land Emigration Office, 9 Park Street, Westminster, re Vessel to be dispatched to South Australia about the 31st March, in which free passages will be granted to a few Agricultural Labourers and Shepherds etc. If you have any eligible persons to propose, the Commissioners will be happy to consider their applications.[xliii]

30 July 1850, Final list of expenses for the emigration of 35 persons from Pytchley on the *Posthumous*, 20 May, the *Lysander*, 30 May, and the *Constance*, 2 July,- to Adelaide, South Australia. Passage Fares- £228.4.3. Total- £366.7.4. high prices of 1847. Some possessions sold but no real value.[xliv]

Rothwell

On 12 April 1845, the Poor Law Board of Kettering authorized the Parish of Rothwell to raise £12 for 'defraying the expenses of the Emigration of poor persons having settlement in the said Parish.

Rushton

1 May 1849, Kettering Poor Law Authorisation: Churchwardens and Overseers authorized to raise £50 to be paid out of the Poor Rates, as a fund for defraying the expenses of the Emigration of poor persons having settlements in the said Parish. List of what payments can be made to emigrants.[xlv]

Warwickshire

The County in the 19th Century

1. *The Topography*

During the 18th and 19th centuries Warwickshire became one of Britain's foremost industrial counties. The coal fields in the north-west were among the most productive in the country and greatly enhanced the growth of Coventry and Birmingham, which became separate county boroughs in 1889. The growth of Leamington, from 315 in 1801 to 26,713 in 1911, as part of the spa water tourist movement, should also be mentioned. In 1838, the town was renamed Royal Leamington Spa. The south of the county was mainly rural with agriculture the most important employment.

2. *Rivers and Canals*
The River Cherwell, a tributary of the Thames, has its headwaters in the county. The county was also the centre of the national canal system, with major arterial routes, such as the Oxford and Coventry Canals, and later the Grand Union being constructed through the county.

3. *Industry*
In the north-east of the county, the Coventry Canal concentrated industry, including coal mining, quarrying, lime and cement making (also at Rugby on the Oxford Canal), and brick and stone were produced. There were huge quarries at Rugby and Stockton. The needle industry included two large mechanical mills at Alcester and Studley.

4. *Agriculture*
Agriculture provided most of the employment in the south of the county, where it bordered rural Oxfordshire. The Return of Owners of Land in 1873 provided similar results to the other three shires, with 4 great estates over 10,000 acres, including the Earl of Aylesford with 12, 158 acres, the Marquis of Hereford at Ragley, Alcester, with 10,281, Lord Leigh of Stoneleigh Abbey with 14,891, and Lord Willoughby De Broke of Compton Verney with 12,621. There were another 92 estates over 1,000 acres, including the Duke of Buccleuch with 6,881 acres, the Marquis of Northampton of Compton Wynyates with 4,985, Sir Robert Peel, the former Prime Minister, with 3,075, Sir N.W. Throckmorton of Coughton Court with 7,618, and the Earl of Warwick of Warwick Castle with 8,262 acres (see Table 7 and Chapter 6).

Population Changes
Table 6 shows the growth in the population of a sample of villages between 1801 and 1851, Most of them reached their peak by 1851 but some not until 1871. In the period to 1911, the village populations all increased significantly by from 20% to 53%. At the same time, the population in the towns more than doubled, as did the county's population. The sample of villages is mostly taken from ones bordering Oxfordshire.

Table 6
Population in Warwickshire, 1801-1911

Village	1801	1851	1871	1891	1911	Decline% (Note 2)
Banbury Poor Law Union						
Farnborough	241	349	**426**	339	297	30%
Radway (Note 3)	237	344	351	241	266	29%
Shotteswell (Note 3)	218	328	308	228	198	39%
Warmington	395	**523**	412	277	252	51%
Chipping Norton PLU (Oxon)						
Long Compton (Note 3)	757	845	715	606	547	38%
Shipston-on-Stour Poor Law Union						
Brailes (Note 3)	980	1,308	1,285	1,060	809	39%
Butlers Marston (Note 3)	200	294	282	230	218	34%
Tysoe	891	1,049	**1,112**	910	731	34%
Whichford	598	**744**	603	507	343	53%
Southam Poor Law Union						
Burton Dassett	600	703	**721**	632	475	34%
Fenny Compton	383	**802**	657	568	510	36%
Priors Marston	538	**739**	718	554	495	33%
Stratford Poor Law Union						
Charlecote (Note 3)	265	286	254	213	224	32%
Kineton	779	1,023	**1,276**	1,021	1,018	20%
						Growth %
Town						1851-1911
Coventry	16,049	17,208	39,474	53,016	**106,349**	123%
Kenilworth	1,968	3,552	3,880	4,173	**5,776**	62%
Leamington Spa	315	15,724	20,910	23,124	**26,713**	71%
Stratford	2,982	6,456	7,384	**8,626**	8,531	32%
Warwick	5,592	10,973	11,002	**11,905**	11,858	8%
Warwickshire	206,798	475,013	634,183	805,080	1,040,409	119%

Notes

1. **Bold type** = peak population 1801-1911

2. Decline % from peak population.

3. Other Peak Dates

1821	Charlecote	331	1841	Shotteswell	366
1831	Butlers Marston	332	1861	Brailes	1,347
	Long Compton	891		Radway	375

Emigration

General Information
19 January 1833, Notice to Young Women Desirous of Bettering Their Condition by an Emigration to New South Wales

  Hand bill and letter from the Commission of the Refuge from the Destitute, Hackney Road, London: Women must be Unmarried or Widows aged 18-30 and must pay £6 towards the Passage. Letter also comments that many women bear hard on the parochial Funds, or are a burthen to their families, solely from the difficulty of obtaining employment. This is apt to drive them into a vicious course of life.[xlvi]

1834-5, Report to the Colonial Secretary of State

a. The following three ships arrived: 1 May, the *Strathfieldsaye* arrived from Gravesend in Hobart, after 104 days; 10 July, *David Scott* in Sydney; 16 October, *Sarah* in VDL.

b. List of persons who arrived by occupation: 1,563 without Allowance or Bounty, Grand Total 2,345.

c. List of average wages: most per week 4s to 8s but annual for Cooks: men £34.15.0, women £17.10.0; Dairywomen £30.00, Farmers £25.00, Gardeners £40.00, Shepherds £25.00.

d. UK Ports used in 1833-34

To: N.America Colonies	USA	S.Africa	Australia
Liverpool: 718/1,395	13,405/18,440	31/3	1,232/256
London: 1,516/1,163	5,709/5357	484/284	2,083/2,346

Other Information

a. 26 Sep 1834, Letter from Hobart Town confirmed the arrival of the Strathfieldsaye from Gravesend after 104 days. Only one death of a child.

b. 31 January 1835, Free passage on the *Canton* from Gravesend *to* Sydney, with clothing details for 4 weeks in a Small Bag. Also small knife, fork, table and tea spoon, a pewter and a tin plate, and a pint and half-pint tea pot.

c. 9 July1835, Free passage for female emigration to VDL, for single women and widows, age 15-30, on the *Charles Kerr* sailing from Gravesend.[xlvii]

d. March 1840, Poster re Emigration to South Australia. New Emigration Fund offers free passages to a limited number of Married labourers, aged 15-30. Wives also free. If uneligible, must pay £17-20 for Passages - usually last 4 months.[xlviii]

e. 1844, *Emigration to Australia, as offered by Marshall & Edridge*
   To enable respectable persons to proceed to the Australian colonies, viz., ADELAIDE, PORT PHILLIP and SYDNEY. 3 ships offered and other equally

fine ships, similarly fitted etc, will succeed; and sailing on the 1ˢᵗ and 15ᵗʰ of each month from LONDON, and the 11ᵗʰ and 25ᵗʰ from PLYMOUTH. Passengers from Ireland can readily join this Line of Ships at Plymouth.
 A further 24 ships are listed as having already been dispatched on this plan.
A Scale of Provisions for each Adult Steerage Passenger is attached.

Individual Parishes
Banbury (Oxon) Poor Law Union
Ratley
May 1845, to Montreal, Canada: John Oliver, 34, Maria, 27, Job, 4, Hannah, 10 months; Daniel Berry, 22, Anne, 23, Martha, 10 months.[xlix]

Shipston-on-Stour Poor Law Union
Tysoe
The departure of Willliam Ashby {Joseph's grandfather} to the United States in 1876 'turned many a mind towards emigration.' 'It began a talk about Tysoe men who in earlier years had left in ones and twos. Weavers and whitlaws, finding no work at home in the thirties, had carried their skills to the States.' 'Agents of Canada and New Zealand were advertising in the local papers. The Union was advising young men to accept the offered assisted passages.' 'Looking back over the years it could be seen that emigration had taken several of the ablest families.' 'The men and boys who left tended to be the more forceful and bright characters, the darlings of their families. For the village to say good bye to ten, twenty, thirty good fellows seemed a calamity.'[l]

Chapter 5

The Victorian Empire, Agricultural Depressions and Trade Unionism

The Victorian Empire

Emigration is inextricably linked to the growth of the Victorian Empire. By 1837, when Queen Victoria came to the throne, most of the white colonies had long been pressing for self-rule. This was particularly true of Canada, where there was growing agitation against domination from England, and a rebellion in 1837, which was led by the French Canadians of Lower Canada, supported by some Americans. In 1791, the colony of Quebec had been divided into two parts, Upper and Lower from their position on the Ottawa River. Upper Canada was up river, closer to the source, and Lower Canada was down river, closer to the mouth of the great waterway. In 1838, Lord Melbourne's Government sent a special emissary as 'Captain-General, High Commissioner and Governor-in-Chief of all the colonies there.' Lord Lambton, first Earl of Durham, known as Radical Jack, was the man selected. He saw his task as finding a formula to keep Canada, and all such white colonies of the Crown, loyal to the British Empire. As one of the Canadian discontents himself said, he was 'the first statesman to avow a belief in the possibility of a permanent connection between the colonies and the Mother Country'[li]. He produced the Durham Report, which was presented to Parliament in February 1839. In 1841, Lower and Upper Canada were re-named Canada East and Canada West and combined in the Province of Canada, as proposed by Lord Durham.

Sadly, personal opposition to Lord Durham, particularly by Lord Brougham, who protested the illegality of his action in banishing eight principal leaders of the rebellion of 1837, made his position untenable and he had no choice but to resign. In spite of a wave of support for him in all parts of Canada, and from many people in England, his authority had been completely undermined, and his Government abandoned him. Two years later, at the age of 48, Lord Durham died and Lady Durham survived him by only sixteen months. In spite of this failure, Sir Robert Peel, the Tory Prime Minister 1841-6, as noted above, achieved the Repeal of the Corn Laws in 1846, the supreme triumph of Free Trade. However, his government fell and he was replaced by the Whigs under Lord John Russell, with its Colonial Secretary, Lord Grey, Durham's brother-in-law, and the devout Free Trader, Charles Trevelyan, as permanent head of the Treasury.[lii] (See Appendix 2 for further details).

John George Lambton, 1st Earl of Durham, by Charles Turner, after Sir Thomas
Lawrence, mezzotint published 1831 (National Portrait Gallery)

Now at last the Durham Report was accepted as imperial policy, and the ideas
of the Colonial Reformers were vindicated. They believed that systematic
colonization was not merely an opportunity, but a duty: these were the Hungry
Forties, the home population had grown by a half in thirty years, and the right
thing for England was the migration of whole communities, to found their own
British dependencies elsewhere in the world. This was among the most important
documents in the whole history of the Empire. It formulated a new relationship
between London and the white colonies and thus shaped the pattern of the
Victorian Empire as a whole. Its overseas Britons were to be trusted not to break
away from the Crown, but to adhere to it in liberty, and to live in the British way
without coercion, as they would at home. Within twenty years all the bigger white
settlements, like Australia and Canada, would have responsible Governments
and they were to become the homes of the millions who joined 'The Great Exodus'
from 1850 to 1914.[liii] Between 1840 and 1872, about six and a half million people
left the British Isles, most of them agricultural labourers and the rate continued

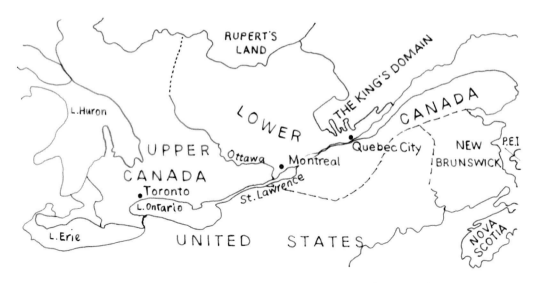

Map of Upper and Lower Canada, 1837-38 (Julie Barrett).

in the 1870s. The pressure slackened after this and an average of 200,000 were going each year in the eighties and nineties. Overall, it has been estimated that 22.6 million left the British Isles 1815-1914.[liv]

These developments were helped by the great technical advances made by the Victorians, notably in shipping and railways. The early shipping of emigrants was all under sail and meant that voyages to Australia could take up to five months. In 1843, however, as noted above, Isambard Brunel built the *SS Great Britain*, 'the ship that changed the world', which was used regularly on the Australasia run and in1861 and 1863 to transport an England Cricket Team to New Zealand. Brunel was also a major contributor to the spread of the railways, and to the building of bridges, including the famous one over the Tamar. The invention of the steam engine, leading to the introduction of steamships, reduced the Australian voyages to 80 days and the Atlantic crossings to 15 days. Improvements continued as people looked for ever increasing speeds but the sailing ship did not die with the coming of steam, at least not at once. The greatest sailing ships ever built emerged in these years [after 1860], and the the fastest of them – the clippers – could sail 400 miles in a day.[lv] The *Cutty Sark* was built specifically to be the fastest clipper on the 'China Tea Run', and was regularly pitted against the *Thermopylae* in the 1870s. In the only directly organized race, *Cutty Sark* was the winner but only because *Thermopylae* lost her rudder. They both managed the Melbourne run in some 60 days and the China run in just over 100 days, so there was no clear winner. The other significant advance was the opening of the Suez Canal in 1869, which cut some 1,000 miles off the run to Australia. The Victorian concentration on ship building also led to the establishment of the strongest navy,

The *Cutty Sark (clipper)* in Sydney Harbour, waiting for the new season's wool,
1885-1894 (National Maritime Museum).

including submarines, and domination of the seas by 1914. At the same time, the
development and spread of the railways after 1850 simplified the access of
emigrants to Liverpool and other ports. It also aided the development of railways
in the colonies. There were also improvements in the handling of the health of
passengers, after the disastrous effects of cholera and typhus on earlier voyages.

There was also a significant milestone in coinage, the Bun Penny, first minted
in 1860. Taking its name from its depiction of the young Queen Victoria, with her
hair in a bun, the 1860 Bun Penny was important in a number of ways. It
introduced bronze for lower denomination UK coins (previously copper). It also
featured a seated Britannia facing right on the reverse and set the dimensions of

The *SS Great Britain*, designed by Isambard Brunel, Bristol, 1843
(National Maritime Museum).

a penny, both features that remained on the penny until 1970. Bun Pennies were minted every year from 1860 to 1894 and during that period Victoria's head was changed subtly as she aged. Whilst pennies were minted throughout the rest of Victoria's reign, in these her portrait has lost the bun and she is shown wearing a veil. There is a Bun Penny pub in Lee-on-Solent and there is thought to be only one other pub with that name in the UK. It is fortunate that there is at least one reminder of this Victorian invention.

Agricultural Depressions

In 1851, agriculture employed over one fifth of the working population and produced about the same proportion of the national income.[lv] 'The years 1840-70 were the 'Golden Age' of English agriculture. Output rose almost as fast as the population, and it is estimated that as late as 1868 80% of the United Kingdom's food was home grown'. Most of the local villages had their peak populations between 1851 and 1871, with a few others before 1851. The agricultural depression of 1874-84 brought an end to the farming boom and caused severe rural poverty. This was aggravated by a second agricultural depression from 1891-99, partly caused by foreign competition, with frozen meat coming in from Australia, New Zealand and South America. Even in Lark Rise, after the Golden Jubilee of 1887, 'nothing ever seemed quite the same.' and 'The Innkeeper's wife got in cases of salmon from Australia and Australian rabbit.'[lvi] There was also growing competition from mass-produced goods and declining local markets, which affected, for example, boot-makers, blacksmiths, tailors and wheelwrights. It also affected women's employment.

These depressions contributed to large numbers moving to towns and emigrating. In August 1872, the Queensland Goverrment took the bold step of offering entirely free passages to approved agricultural labourers and their wives and children, with the virtual certainty of jobs being available for them on arrival. By doing so, Queensland was able to secure large numbers of labourers who could never have afforded to pay even part of their fares themselves. Between 1871 and 1911 six million Britons emigrated, with the peak in the 1870s and 1890s. Most of them were men from rural areas, so that by 1900 there were over one million more women than men in Britain. Advertisements in the *Bicester Advertiser* at the time included many offers of free land in Canada, New Zealand and Australia. By 1901, however, Canada was 'the only country offering free land to home seekers of limited means.' No less than 50,000 per annum were entering her ports. In many cases the parishes also gave some support, as they had done earlier in the nineteenth century. In addition, by the late 1890s, men with any ambition in the villages were looking for wider opportunities in factories, on the railways and docks and in the new urban police forces.

By the 1870s, conditions were more favourable for large-scale organizations, like the industrial unions. In 1871 in Oxfordshire, 23,220 males were employed in agriculture. By 1911, there were 15,128. In 1901, Rider Haggard was told by the schoolmaster in Greater Rollright that 'three quarters of the young men and all the young women left the village at nineteen or twenty years of age, only the dullest staying at home.' By 1901, agriculture employed less than a tenth of the labour force and its share of national income was less than a fifteenth. In its reduced role, farming became a more harshly commercial business. There was a major shift to pasture, a fall in sheep numbers and an increase in cattle. The least profitable arable farming was abandoned and the labour force cut back. The most able farmers deserted the land, even left the country altogether. By 1907, the Oxfordshire weekly agricultural wage was the lowest in England and Wales at 14s.11d. The isolation and ignorance of the country worker were gradually breaking down. As time went by, railways, visits to towns, newspapers, the penny post, and the activities of emigration agents all tended to bring the rural worker into the current of contemporary life.

Agricultural Trade Unionism[lvii]

There was sporadic union activity in a number of counties in the 1860s but agricultural labourers came relatively late to the idea of trade unionism. It was not until the end of a period of prosperity for English agriculture in the 1860s that they saw the possible benefits which trade unionism could bring. On 14 February

1872, Joseph Arch addressed the men of Wellesbourne 'under the chestnut tree' and he was chosen to head the Warwickshire union, and a large number of other separate organizations sprung up. In Oxfordshire, the focus of discontent was Milton-under-Wychwood which formed the Milton Union. The main aim of the new unions was to secure an extension of the franchise to rural householders (not achieved until 1884), and improved wages and conditions of employment but some of the leaders quickly began to see emigration as a means of indirectly bringing this about. In 1873, the National Agricultural Labourers Union (NALU) was formed out of these local organizations, with Joseph Arch as President. It was Milton-under-Wychwood which provided the nucleus of the Oxford District of NALU.

In 1873, 16 women of Ascott-under–Wychwood were sent to prison for the part they played in the founding of NALU. Mr Hambridge of Crown Farm, Ascott, sacked his men who had joined the Union and then employed men from Ramsden. The women stopped the Ramsden men working and tried to persuade them to join the Union. They were charged with obstruction and coercion and tried in Chipping Norton. The ringleaders were sentenced to imprisonment with hard labour, seven of them for 10 days, and nine women for 7 days. There was a violent riot with some 1,000 people swarming round the Police Court. The women were taken to Oxford Prison. During the women's absence in prison their children were cared for by kind neighbours and the officials of the Milton-under-Wychwood branch of the Workers Union. Mary Pratley, one of the women, later emigrated with her husband, Frederick, and his brother, Eli, with his wife and daughter. They sailed on the *Ballochmyle* to Christchurch, New Zealand (see Chapter 6).

Initially, Arch was 'inimical to emigration movements amongst the agricultural class.' But he and other leaders came to see that by emigration, local surpluses of labour could be eliminated, and the bargaining position of those who remained behind would be strengthened. So this led to the development of union-sponsored emigration. By the summer of 1873, Arch had accepted an invitation from the Canadian Government, with a view to considering its suitability for union emigration. His tour, which lasted until November, also included a brief visit to the United States. In Canada he received a very warm welcome, as the *Ottawa Times* noted '…the visit of Mr Arch is of no small importance. We want, and grievously want, the very class that Mr Arch represents.' In 1872-3, real interest in emigration among farm workers became apparent and, as noted above, it was Queensland which proved most able to take advantage of it. In March 1873, in Swanbourne, near Winslow, following a strike of agricultural labourers, nearly all of them accepted the terms offered by Sir Thomas Fremantle, the major land owner. These required them to resign from the newly formed NALU, which most of them did in spite of a visit from Joseph Arch. A few of them looked at the possibility of emigration and at least three eventually went to Queensland.[lviii]

Edward Richardson, known later as the Aylesbury Agitator, had been a schoolmaster but when the agricultural union movement (NALU) developed in Buckinghamshire during 1872, he soon became fully involved in recruitment for it. He proved particularly effective and his agency work for the Queensland Government followed on from this, for which he seems to have been well paid. He made his agency headquarters at the appropriately named Brisbane House in Aylesbury. At the same time, a Queenslander by adoption and of much experience in the colony, Richard Daintree, was sent home to London as Agent General with authority to engage sub-agents in Britain. Richardson approached him with a proposal to assemble a large party of out-of-work labourers to take advantage of these free offers and he would accompany them. Daintree accepted and Richardson accompanied a couple of large parties to Queensland (see under Aylesbury below).

Richardson severed his connections with emigration after this because of financial problems with the Queensland Government which claimed that he owed them £155 18s.5d. The Colonial Secretary stated that this amount 'may be written off' and went on to state that 'Mr Richardson is not a person in whom any reliance can be placed and ...he is utterly undeserving of the confidence of the Government.' He had an unhappy career after this, ending up in a fatal boating accident in Macquarrie Harbour in Tasmania on 4 May 1878. Immediately prior to his death, he had been working as an actor and free-lance journalist in Hobart, Tasmania. It does appear from subsequent examination that Richardson was not guilty of the charges brought against him.

In 1872, Wootton was also a centre of agricultural unrest, with an early branch of NALU formed in May 1872. It was led by Chris Holloway, the Chairman of the Oxford District of the National Union, demanding an increase in wages from 11s to 16s per week. About 120 labourers withdrew their labour, and some moved to Sheffield. In 1873, he and Henry Taylor were hired by the New Zealand authorities to act as agents to select suitable migrants and accompany them all the way to New Zealand. They received twice the rates of pay of an average farm worker and their expenses for undertaking this role. They used their standing among the agricultural communities of Warwickshire and Oxfordshire to attract migrants. The contingent set off from Leamington on 13 December 1873, picking up a further group from Tysoe at Banbury, and yet more emigrants at Oxford, including villagers from Wootton. By the time they reached Plymouth, there were 700 men, women and children in the party.

They set sail in two vessels of the New Zealand Shipping Company, the steamer *Mongol* and the sailing ship *Scimitar* on 23 and 24 December 1873 to

By Authority of H. M. 🦁🦁 Government of Queensland.

EMIGRATION TO QUEENSLAND, AUSTRALIA.

From the great demand which now exists in the Colony for all kinds of labour, the Agent-General will grant

FREE PASSAGES

TO

FARM-LABOURERS & FEMALE DOMESTIC SERVANTS,

(Without undertaking for payment of cost of passage,)

AND

ASSISTED PASSAGES

TO

MECHANICS AND OTHER ELIGIBLE PERSONS.

TO INTENDING EMIGRANTS.

An unusual opportunity now presents itself to Farm-Labourers, Female Domestic Servants, and other eligible Persons desirous of Emigrating to Queensland, under the personal superintendence of Mr. E. RICHARDSON (of Aylesbury), who has made official arrangements to accompany some 300 emigrants on or about the 17th of March next.

The advantages offered are a Free Passage, Free Kit, and Railway Fare Paid. Each emigrant being required to provide the regulation quantity of clothing only. Special advantages offered to Female Servants. The increased demand for good servants has materially improved the rates of wages, which now stand as follows: Female Domestic Servants from £30 to £52 per annum. General Labourers from £30 to £50 per annum. Ploughmen from £60 to £70 per annum; with rations, consisting of 8lbs. of flour; 12lbs. of beef; 2lbs. of sugar; ¼lb. tea—weekly.

Mr. Richardson expects to return to England about November, 1873, to report upon the prospects of New Settlers in Queensland. He will also visit those persons who left Aylesbury for Brisbane, in the ship ' Storm King.'

Gentry and friends can render valuable assistance by helping bona-fide emigrants with gifts of wearing apparel, also by assisting in filling up the necessary forms.

As the responsibility of this undertaking is necessarily great, Mr. Richardson will gladly acknowledge, on behalf of the emigrants, any pecuniary help, parcels of left-off clothing, books, or other articles needed during a long voyage.

An early and personal application (if possible) should be made to Mr. E. RICHARDSON, or Mr. S. G. PAYNE, Government Agent, Aylesbury.

L. POULTON, PRINTER, MARKET SQUARE, AYLESBURY.

Emigration to Queensland with Mr E.Richardson - official notice, 1873 (Queensland Record Office).

Dunedin. The job of Taylor and Holloway was only complete after their arrival in New Zealand in early March 1874 and clearing quarantine. After this, Holloway spent several months touring all parts of New Zealand. In Spring 1875, after his return to England, he became 'a special travelling agent' of the New Zealand Government. From 1877 until April 1880, he seems to have been paid an annual salary of about £150. Then there was a general depression and emigration to New Zealand was curtailed and Holloway took a grocer's shop in his native Wootton.

In 1872-3, Charles Carter, who worked closely with the unions, held meetings in the Wychwoods and recruited considerable numbers to go and work for Brogdens, the rail contractors, in New Zealand (see Chapter 6). On 28 February 1874, a group of some 200 Oxfordshire labourers sailed from Plymouth to Canterbury, New Zealand, on the *Ballochmyle*, led by Joseph Legget, secretary of the Oxford District of NALU, and a former carpenter from Milton-under-Wychwood. But by 1874, farmers were replying to union demands with lockouts, blackleg labour and eviction of union supporters from their cottages. From this point onwards its membership began to decline and by 1879 little remained of the enthusiasm seven years before. 'The 'revolt of the field' had failed and its leaders turned to political action. NALU's membership had fallen from over 86,000 in 1874 to 15,000 by the end of 1881 and by 1889 was a mere 4,254. Although Joseph Arch went on to become Liberal member of Parliament for a Norfolk seat, the Union faded into obscurity in the 1890s and was finally dissolved in 1896. However, it is clear that it, particularly at its height in the period 1872-5, did encourage emigration of farm workers from Britain. There are no reliable NALU emigration statistics available but it is estimated that perhaps 40,000 to 45,000 unionists and their families might have been sponsored by NALU to emigrate during the period 1872-81; this assumes that each male emigrant would, on average, be accompanied by three dependants.[lix]

In the period 1871-80, 41,449 adult male agricultural labourers, shepherds, carters, gardeners etc. were officially reported to have left Britain with their families. In the previous decade 1861-70, the total was a mere 17,434. It seems that most of the emigrants were satisfied with their move and that some of the union officials who escorted parties out to the colonies also decided to settle there, notably Joseph Leggett, the Oxford district secretary, in New Zealand, and Henry Taylor, the first general secretary of NALU, in South Australia. As for the agricultural unions, after 1881 they virtually ceased to play any part at all in the sponsored emigration of their members.[lx] NALU had no further involvement in emigration and among the agricultural classes it was encouraged only by non-union emigration agents and under the influence of seemingly better economic prospects overseas, particularly in the United States.

Nonconformists

As noted above, a significant number of the Cornish emigrants to Australia, particularly to South Australia, were Wesleyans, Primitive Methodists and Bible Christians - the last group a Methodist denomination founded in North Cornwall in 1815. They all sought to recreate their religious communities overseas, at a time when there was great enthusiasm and growth in Dissent in England. By the 1850s, 'at least half of the population [of Australia] were Irish Catholics, Scottish Presbyterians or Cornish Methodists'. There was also another interesting link with the Nonconformists in Tasmania, which I found on a trip to Australia. The unusual fingerpost in Sheffield, Tasmania, includes directions to the Garden of Eden, Paradise and the Promised Land. These places were given biblical names by Reuben Austin, J.H.Dawson and other Christian Brethren, when they were walking on the foothills of Mt Roland, near Sheffield in the 1870s. It is remarkable that over thirty biblical place names are found here within a few square kilometres, including Zion Hill, Damascus Gate and Devil's Gullet. They immediately conjure up visions of Christian's journey in *Pilgrim's Progress*. The Brethren seem to have been devout Calvinists but their leader, Reuben Austin, was apparently fond of reading the published sermons of Charles Spurgeon

Nonconformist Finger Post, Sheffield, Tasmania, including the 'Promised Land', (the author).

(1834-92). He was the outstanding preacher of his generation and was described by Chadwick as 'the young genius who strengthened the impact of dissent and of the Baptists upon the nation'.[lxii] Interestingly too, a recent book about the Christian pioneers in Tasmania is titled 'Spurgeon's Men: The Resurgence of Baptist Belief and Practice in Tasmania, 1869-1884'. The influence of Spurgeon and Bunyan clearly spread far beyond Spurgeon's Metropolitan Tabernacle at the Elephant & Castle, and Bunyan's Bedford Church. They, and the Christian Brethren, exemplify the enthusiasm and commitment of the various Nonconformist sects, and the part they played in the development of Australia.

Chapter 6

The Great Exodus, 1850-1914

The Great Exodus

Until after 1850, poverty, custom and ignorance kept country labourers set in their ways. Their ignorance was profound and this limited migration. As late as 1866 in North Devon, for example, Canon Girdlestone was moving labourers to industrial towns in the north, and he had to consign them to the railways like parcels![lxiii] The leaders were clergymen, landowners, and village emigration societies, whose members paid into a fund until there was enough to draw lots and decide which family was to go. Also agents of shipping companies, American railroads, land companies, and state governments placed advertisements in newspapers, held public meetings and generally roused interest in emigration.

If a villager emigrated, made good and wrote back to relatives and friends, the impact could be considerable. There were high emigration figures from 1852 to 1867, averaging 198,000 a year, some of them assisted by the Colonial Land and Emigration Commissioners, founded in 1847, and the bulk of them making for Australasia. 'Early in the century [Australia] was the convict hell, somewhere nobody would go voluntarily. But then as free settlement became dominant, it suddenly became the place to send people for redemption. Charles Dickens, for example, sent two of his sons, Edward, nicknamed 'Plorn' and Alfred, in the 1860s. 'Plorn, who had struggled at a number of schools, was shipped out in 1868 in order to, in the words of his father, "apply himself".'[lxiv] From 1853 to 1880, some 2.8 million left the UK, while between 1853 and 1913, some 13 million emigrated, most of them farm labourers. 'Whole families and groups of families went together, spurred on by the posters and advertisements which had long decorated their cottage walls.' The decade from 1871 to 1881 saw a 140 per cent increase in the number of farm labourers, shepherds, gardeners and carters who moved abroad.

It is worth noting that the *Bicester Advertiser* of 22 November 1901 said that Canada was 'now the only country offering free land to home seekers of limited means. 50,000pa enter her ports, 75% go at once to the North West Territories.' In 1904, a 32 page pamphlet, called 'Canada in a Nutshell', was produced by WTR Preston, Commissioner of Emigration, based in London. It included the following information:

a. The following classes who should emigrate:

1. Farmers or persons with experience on farms
2. Men who have been accustomed to hard work and who have pluck and ambition to succeed.
3. Persons without agricultural experience determined to devote themselves to it.

b. No assisted passages, Good Wages and Desirable Homes immediately on arrival, and Advice from Canadian Government officials and reputable booking agents.

c. Immigration figures for Canada, 1896 16,825, and 1903, 134,370, and for Winnipeg, 1880, 6,178, 1890, 25,000, and 1903, 134,370.

d. Offers: 160 acres free grant fertile prairie land- for every head (of household) and son of 18. Land West of Lake Superior and East of the Rocky Mountains [a range of at least 2,000 miles!].

The major surges in emigration were in 1879-93 and in 1903-14. By 1910, nearly half a million people a year (including those Europeans who left via British ports) were leaving the British Isles, although it should be noted that over one million came home in 1911-14. Many of the emigrants saw it as a search for 'The Promised Land', and land had often been on offer from the colonies. At the same time, a great many country folk moved into towns.

Return of Owners of Land, 1873

The Return of Owners of Land in 1873 (otherwise known as the Modern Domesday Survey) was compiled in response to allegations that the 1861 Census showed that there were no more than 30,000 landowners and that they constituted a harmful monopoly. The Local Government Boards were ordered in 1872 to compile a return from rating records. The Return failed predictably to convince either side of the debate. However, the Returns for the Four Shires do reveal the dominance of a comparatively small number of landowners. They also reveal a similarity between them, although Northamptonshire has a significantly larger figure for owners between 3,000 and 9,999 acres (For a summary of the results see Table 7). It is also worth mentioning that the number of large landowners in the 1840s must have been very much the same when the battle was raging over the Repeal of the Corn Laws, and it was opposed by most of them (see above).

We look below at the effect of the Great Exodus on Oxfordshire and its neighbouring shires.

Table 7
Return of Owners of Land in the Four Shires, 1873

Oxfordshire				Number	Acres
Total Owners of land above one acre				3,344	448,406
Toatl owners of land less than one acre				6,833	876
Estimated commons or waste lands					2,949
				10,177	452,232
Buckinghamshire					
Total Owners of land above one acre				3,288	455,056
Toatl owners of land less than one acre				6,420	1,153
Estimated commons or waste lands					2,942
				9,708	459,151
Northamptonshire					
Total Owners of land above one acre				4,455	589,748
Toatl owners of land less than one acre				10,010	3,022
Estimated commons or waste lands					254
				14,465	593,026
Warwickshire					
Total Owners of land above one acre				4,622	535,137
Toatl owners of land less than one acre				46,894	5,883
Estimated commons or waste lands					1,833
				51,516	542,855

Analysis of Owners of Land over 1,000 acres					
				Oxfordshire	Buckinghamshire
Over 10,000 acres			1	21,944	2	26,620
3,000 to 9,999 acres			20	105,360	22	107,290
1,000 to 2,999 acres			74	127,875	59	103,006
			95	255,179	83	236,916
Percentage of total			0.93%	56%	0.85%	48%

			Northamptonshire		Warwickshire	
Over 10,000 acres			5	81,751	4	49,951
3,000 to 9,999 acres			28	142,189	21	101,026
1,000 to 2,999 acres			71	116,262	71	119,543
			104	340,202	96	270,520
Percentage of total			0.71%	57%	0.2%	49%

Oxfordshire

Return of Owners of Land, 1873

The survey shows that there was only one great estate over 10,000 acres in the county, the Duke of Marlborough at Blenheim Park with 21,944 acres, which included significant holdings in West Oxfordshire. The greater gentry included the Earl of Abingdon at Wytham with 8,173 acres, Matthew Boulton at Tew Park with 7,945 acres (he was grandson of the famous engineer, partner of James Watt), Sir Henry Dashwood at Kirtlington with 7,515 acres, and the Earl of Jersey at Middleton Park with 7,042 acres.

Population Changes

Table 3 shows the significant percentage decline in the population of a selection of Oxfordshire villages from 1851 to 1911, from 11% up to 44%. Table 2 shows how the populations of Banbury and Oxford increased by 64% and 74%, and the population of Oxfordshire by 11%, with 72% urban growth but a decline of 6% in the rural population.

Emigration

At a local level, in the late nineteenth century, emigration was clearly a topic for discussion, for example in Juniper, where some relatives of Emma Timms, Flora Thompson's mother, who had settled in New South Wales and were on a visit to England, 'nearly persuaded Nurse Emma to go back with them.' Indeed, it was all settled until, one night, they began to talk about snakes and Emma changed her mind. 'I shan't go, for I can't abear [sic] the horrid creatures.' But 'of the next generation her second son [Frank] became a fruit farmer in Queensland and of the next a son of Laura's [Henry Basil] is now an engineer in Brisbane.'[lxii] The personal experiences of a Fringford family, the Butlers, also shed some interesting light on emigration. As noted below, Henry and three of his brothers emigrated to Queensland from 1869-74. Their story illustrates both the trials and the rewards for those prepared to try it, and why it could be preferable to working in England in this period (see Chapter 8).

Individual Parishes

Banbury Poor Law Union
Banbury
17 March 1887, the *Banbury Guardian* reported a sad sign of the times. 'Yesterday morning upwards of sixty emigrants left the GWR Station for Liverpool, en route for America. They came from villages in the neighbourhood, including Warmington, Ratley, Sibford, Epwell, Middleton Cheney, Chacombe, Farthinghoe, Souldern and Deddington.'[lxiii]

There are also the following examples of emigrant mobility:

a. Sarah Beesley (1812-92) kept in touch with her sister Harriet in Melbourne. In 1864 and 1877 she sent parcels to her with young emigrating Banburians. In 1892, aged 68, after the deaths of her husband and son-in-law, Harriet returned to Banbury, more than 40 years after she left. In 1878, Sarah's sister, Elizabeth, aged 60, returned with a cousin, Russell Wlikins, and his family on the *SS Hankow* to Melbourne.

b. Thomas Gunn (1826-1904), several of his cousins went to Australia, as did his cousin, Henry Gunn, from South Newington. He subsequently crossed the Pacific to California to prospect for gold. Thomas Gunn himself made a living in New York literary and artistic circles.[lxiv]

Bloxham
In 1887, £2 was paid to a man to go to Droitwich, £6.2s 6d to help one emigrate to Canada and £10 to a family for the same purpose.

18 Jan 1859, Elizabeth Needle, deserted wife of David Needle, and children under 10, to join him in Canada.

Little Bourton
2 April 1852, 4 persons (un-named) to Quebec, Canada by the *Ava*.

6 Aug 1852, To Sydney, Australia: William Lincoln, 29, Caroline, 24, Henry, 2, Charlotte Sharman, 4.

Claydon
2 Sep 1852, To Sydney, Australia: Charles Duckett, 19, wife, Hannah, 29, Mary Ann Nicholls, 2 (illegitimate child of Hannah Duckett).

Hanwell
4 Nov 1852, To Sydney, Australia: Elias John Painter, 34, Hannah, 39, Sarah Elizabeth, 4.

Wroxton
21 April 1851, To Quebec, Canada, the following embarked on the *Sisters*, 28 May 1851: Thomas Hall, 33, single; Eli Jecock, 25, single; Frederick Hall, 22; single, Richard Lucas, 22, single; Unni Lucas, 17, single; John Allington, 17, single.

17 Oct 1851, To Port Phillip, NSW (sailed 3 Dec): George Marriott, 22, Charlotte (formerly Nicholls), 22, William Nicholls, 2.

Bicester Poor Law Union

Bicester

In 1910, George Shaw (1881-1962), with his wife and daughter, emigrated to Junee, near Katoomba, NSW. Sadly, his son, Cyril, died of whooping cough on the voyage and was buried in Cape Town, South Africa. George set up a thriving butcher's business in Junee, where he was elected mayor several years running.

In 1913, Arthur Edward Waine travelled to Canada via New York. After working on a potato farm at Thornhill, Ontario, he went north to the mining township of Nairns Centre, where he became deputy Sheriff for the Algoma region. From 1919 to 1944, he ran a very successful business in the North York district of Willowdale, as a gravel trucker and mover of wooden houses.[lxv]

Fringford

By the mid-1850s, Thomas Simons (1831-71). a farmer, had emigrated to Buenos Aires, Argentina. The very recent discovery of the gravestone of his eldest son, also Thomas, in Fringford, revealed that he had been born in Buenos Ayres (sic) but died at Bicester in 1869. Further research revealed that in 1856 his father married Eliza Jane Malcolm (1837-93), who had been born in Buenos Aires. Their son, Thomas, was born there in 1857 and four more siblings were born there from 1861-65, although three seem to have died young. The family must have returned to England soon after that, as Harry was born in Bicester in 1868. In the 1871 census, Thomas was described as 'a proprietor of land', and he and Eliza were living in Market End, Bicester, with John, aged 7 and Harry aged 3 but Thomas died there later that year. Harry returned to Buenos Aires but Eliza and John both stayed in England and she died in 1893 in Bedford. Thomas's older brother, John (1827-96), farmed at Manor Farm, Fringford, succeeding his father, Thomas, in the 1850s.

It seems likely that Eliza Malcolm's parents emigrated sometime after Argentina declared its independence from Spain in 1816. The early emigrants from the United Kingdom were mostly educated and prosperous and making the most of fresh opportunities. Later, there was a fresh wave of emigrants, with 2,708 from the United Kingdom in the 1860s, and by 1869 Argentina had the second largest number of immigrants, with 6.6 million or 11% of the population, and 50% of Buenos Aires were newly arrived emigrants. In the 1870s, the number from the United Kingdom increased to 9,265 and in the 1880s to 15,692. So Thomas Simons seems to have been an early member of the Great Exodus.

The Butler Family

In 1827, as noted above, 'John Butler and his eldest son, Reuben, were transported to Australia on the *Prince Regent.* ' John's nephew, Richard, was a cordwainer (shoemaker) in Fringford, married to Rhoda (Thame). They had 12 children of whom four died in infancy, and four sons emigrated to Australia, Henry, Joseph, Charles and Thomas. Henry had moved from Fringford to Liverpool in the late 1850s, where he worked on the railway.

Joseph (1848-1909) was the first brother to emigrate, sailing from Gravesend on the *Royal Dane* on 9 December 1869, and landing at Rockhampton, Queensland. It seems likely that he had left Fringford earlier to join his brother, Henry, in Liverpool working on the railway. No doubt they were both attracted to the idea of emigrating to Queensland by stories circulating in Liverpool, the Gateway to the Empire. Queensland had become a separate colony in 1859, breaking away from New South Wales (NSW), and it was very keen to attract emigrants. Joseph, as the unmarried brother, no doubt agreed to go first, His first job in Australia was as an engine driver in Brisbane, presumably based on his experience in Liverpool.

Henry (1834-1924), with his wife and four young children, sailed from Gravesend on 30 July 1870 on the *Royal Dane* arriving at Rockhampton on 19 November 1870. No doubt he had been reassured by his brother, Joseph's experience. They were due to go to Brisbane but the Government of NSW ordered the ship and immigrants further north to Rockhampton to increase the settlement there. There was little work available there, so he moved further north to Mackay, after two years to Townsville, and then to Magnetic Island.

Charles (1852-1946) sailed from London on 25 July 1874 on the *Darling Downs* and arrived in Brisbane on 5 November 1874, closely followed by

Thomas (1856-1948), who sailed from London on 13 September 1874 on board the *Indus*, arriving in Brisbane on 29 December 1874; they were both on assisted passages. They both joined Henry on Magnetic Island.[lxvi] (see also Chapter 8).

Fritwell

24 June 1874, Raymus (31) and Martha (29) Butler, with 5 children aged from 4 months to 11, boarded the *Cartvale* from the New Zealand Emigration Depot at Brunswick Wharf, Blackwall. They were towed to Gravesend and on the following morning they were towed by tug out to open sea. The ship reached Wellington Heads on 9 October and was towed into the harbour on the 10 October after a voyage of 106 days. Even then the voyage and the drama was not yet over.

Due to the number of deaths on board (19), the *Cartvale* was immediately

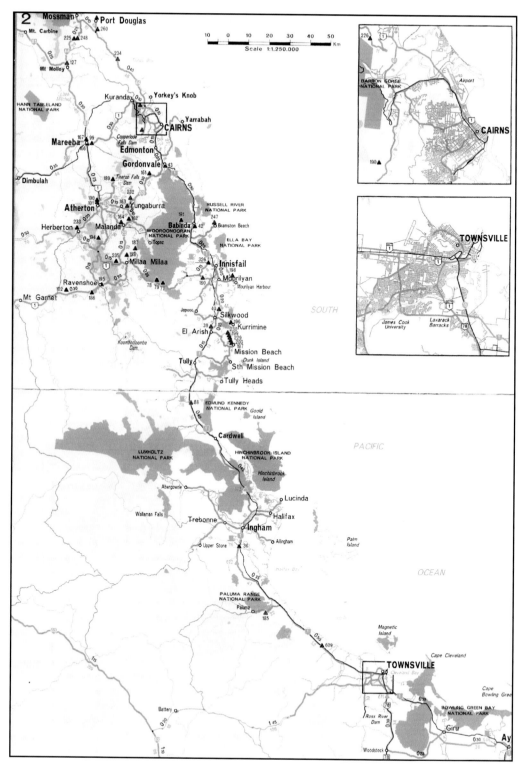

Map of Northern Queensland (Grace Rutherford).

sent to Somes Island, the quarantine station in the middle of Wellington Harbour. This was followed by over 30 deaths on the next emigrant ship, the *Douglas*, and a Commission of Enquiry was convened to investigate. The officers and crew were exonerated, with much of the blame laid on the poor physical condition of the passengers. However, the ship's owners were seriously criticised for failing to provide adequate and suitable stores and rations for the voyage. By 1881, Raymus had acquired his own farm, a Crown Grant in the new settlement of Manaia in the Province of Taranaki, on the west coast of North Island.[lxvii]

Lower Heyford
About 1860, the village's fortunes began to decline. In 1850, 3 inhabitants were assisted to emigrate to Canada. The population declined from 625 in the peak years of 1861-71 to 494 in 1901. It was still only 398 in 1951.

Islip
On 10 April 1874, the *Stonehouse* set sail from Plymouth for Christchurch, New Zealand, with James Beckley and his wife, Caroline, and children, Charley and Edwin, on board. The voyage lasted 80 days and saw the death of 23 children but not the Beckleys'. James wrote his letter or footnote to his son and family immediately after docking in Christchurch. He is clearly not in the least downhearted and will not let the green grass of New Zealand grow under his feet: 'A sheep costs 13 shillings. A cow £4 8s. A calf from £4 up to £10.' He prospered.[lxviii]

Juniper Hill, Cottisford
In January 1912, Frank Timms, brother of Flora, emigrated on the *Demosthenes* to Sydney. He was a fruit farmer in Cooran, Queensland until his death in April 1952.

In about 1913, Edwin Timms, another of Flora's brothers, emigrated to Canada, probably to the Prairies as he signed up in 1914 in Winnipeg to join the Canadian Infantry (Eastern Ontario Regiment). He died in Belgium on 26 April 1916, aged 36 and is buried in Zillebeke (just south of Ypres).[lxix]

Launton
In 1852, the Bicester Board of Guardians sanctioned £32 for emigration to Australia of poor persons from Launton. The population of the village declined from a peak of 746 in 1871 to 544 in 1911.

In 1855, Thomas and John Freeman emigrated from Launton to Australia and, like the Addinsalls from Leamington (see below) settled in Muddy Creek,

Victoria. They were also Nonconformists and on 26 December, 1858, they were involved in the opening of a new union church, free to all Protestant denominations. John Addinsall and Richard Burgin were involved, as Free Methodists, while the Freemans were Congregationalists, and others were Primitive Methodists, Wesleyan Methodists, and Baptists.[lxx]

On 21 March 1867, John Freeman wrote to the Editor of the *Bicester Herald* from Hamilton, Victoria. 'We have gathered in an abundant harvest and of a truth can say that we have bread for the eater and seed for the sower.' He also comments about the problems for farmers and the alarming bush fires. 'The changes in this country are rapid, and so that all new emigrants will have to give a long price for land, or go a long way into the interior. Going 100 miles in this country is thought no more of than going from Bicester to Oxford. We are all well and possess all that reasonable men should wish. Please receive £1 from the order enclosed as my subscription to the *Bicester Herald*, and oblige by forwarding the other £1 to the Building Committee of the Congregational School, Water Lane.'[lxxi]

Chipping Norton Poor Law Union

The Wychwood Villages (named after the Forest)

In 1857-59, disafforestation meant the loss of woodmen's jobs and an increase of farm labourers. The villagers' grazing rights were replaced by small commons around the forest edge. Initially this and the construction of the railway led to an increase in the population of 84% between 1811 and 1871. However, these commons predictably were on the poorest land and within 5 years all had been separately enclosed. As the benefit of the construction and arrival of the railway also dried up, coupled with the slump in agriculture, the population declined by 26% between 1871 and 1911, with many seeking to emigrate or move to industrial areas of this country.

In July 1872, Charles Carter, as emigration agent supporting Brogden & Sons, as noted above, held a meeting in Shipton-under-Wychwood. He recruited ten families, who left on 13 September 1872 and arrived in Napier, Hawkes Bay, on 28 December. Brogdens guaranteed these emigrants two years of work on Brogden railway construction at not less than 5s per day (about twice the UK agricultural rate) with the costs of fares to London for emigration, ship's 'kit' and the voyage all met by the company. The recruits promised to pay Brogdens £16 per adult at a future date.

John Brogden met the first shipment of recruits as they reached Wellington and transferred to a coastal steamer for the last part of their journey to Picton, across the Cook Strait, on the tip of the South Island. He tried to get them to settle for minimum wages but they refused to agree anything less than 6s for a

9-hour day. In fact, 8 hour days were already the norm in New Zealand. Even so, the recruits sent letters home with glowing reports about the good wages and hours. By August 1873, 2,172 immigrants had been brought out. They included 1,299 working-age men who were contracted to work for Brogdens for two years but only 287 of them were still working for them. Most of the men were agricultural labourers, rather than true navvies, and they found agricultural labour and working conditions more attractive than navvy work.

In 1873, New Zealand offered free passages for suitable emigrants, and there was an immediate response. In November 1873, 500-600 were present in a large marquee which was used frequently for chapel and union functions in Milton-under-Wychwood, owned by Isaac Castle. Carter's speech lasted one hour and 40 minutes on the wonders of life in New Zealand. A collection of £17 was made to help a group about to leave for Hawkes Bay on the *Inverene*. A hundred adults and children left Milton (Nov-Dec 1873). According to shipping records, they included Thomas Turner with his large family; also several large inter-related families, many of them active in the agricultural union movement and Nonconformist chapels. For the success of some of this group in New Zealand see Chapter 8. However, the company found that work was slower than expected and in 1879 they were in dispute with the New Zealand Government over contract payments. Bankruptcy soon followed.

In November 1873, Eli Pratley returned to Ascott-under-Wychwood from America with his family, all in wretched condition. In February 1874, his half brother John's son Philip left for New Zealand with his wife and three children, presumably on the *Ballochmyle* which sailed to Canterbury, NZ. Eli himself re-married on 16 May 1874 and emigrated for the second time in September. This time he emigrated to New Zealand with his new wife, and a daughter aged 5. His brother, Frederick, was on the same ship, with his wife, Mary Ann, who had been one of the Ascott Martyrs (see above), and 6 children. In 1873, 16 women of Ascott-under-Wychwood were sent to prison. Both prospered farming on the South Island, initially on a joint lease, and later on separate farms. Eli had ten sons and one daughter.[lxxii]

On 17 November1874, as noted above, the '*Cospatrick*' disaster occurred. The ship embarked at the Blackwall emigrant depot near London with 470 passengers and crew and sailed for Auckland on 11 September 1874. There were only three survivors, members of the crew, when the ship caught fire on 17 November 1874, 250 miles west of the Cape of Good Hope. Seven local residents were lost, all members of the families of Richard Hedges and Henry Townsend. Four years later, a stone memorial fountain was erected on the village green at Shipton-under-Wychwood to commemorate the community's tragic loss. After this disaster, local interest in emigration waned.[lxxiii]

Headington Poor Law Union
Cuddesdon
In the late 19th century, emigration was fostered, with eighty villagers sailing together for Queensland on one occasion.

Oxford
25 April 1853, Alfred Joy and his new wife, Henrietta Julia Carlina Solari (born c.1829). sailed from Gravesend in the barque *Thamas Harrison*, with 17 unassisted passengers on board, including 13 'tween-deck passengers', and the Surgeon, Frederick George Howard (32). The voyage lasted 155 'tedious days', according to his diary, docking in Melbourne on 22 September 1853. There are more details from his diary in Chapter 8.[lxxiv]

Thame Poor Law Union
Great Milton
An Emigration Fund was set up and raised about £50 by 1870 to send a group to join an immigration party going from London to Quebec and Markham in Canada. Free rail journeys in Canada and employment were promised.

Witney Poor Law Union
Clanfield
There was active support for emigration by the Vestry. During the agricultural depressions of the 1870s and 1880s, there was a sharp fall in the population from 602 in 1871 to 429 in 1891.

South Leigh
In the 1860s and early 1870s, there was a sharp fall in the population, largely due to emigration. At least 12 families emigrated to New Zealand and in 1878 all but two of the farms were vacant. (Note: in 1848 there were six farms with over 100 acres).

Stanton Harcourt
The population fell from 624 in 1871 to 541 in 1881, probably largely through emigration, as at South Leigh.

Witney
In the late 1850s, when 'a large number' from the Witney area were 'anxious to avail themselves' of the opportunity; applications were invited by an emigration agent based on Church Green. The population also fell in the 1850s and 1860s, partly through emigration.

Woodstock Poor Law Union

Deddington

In the 19th century, there was recurrent poverty, and emigration was encouraged in the 1880s, when Deddington was described as a 'dead-alive place'.

Steeple Aston

Migration to manufacturing districts in England or abroad was promoted by the Vestry. In 1852, they agreed to offer £3 each to up to 8 people who would be prepared to emigrate.

Wootton

As noted above, in 1872, Wootton was a centre of agricultural unrest, led by Chris Holloway and Henry Taylor. They assembled a group which, by the time they reached Plymouth, numbered 700 men, women and children. They set sail in two vessels of the New Zealand Shipping Company, the steamer *Mongol* and the sailing ship *Scimitar* on 23 and 24 December 1873 to Dunedin The job of Taylor and Holloway was only complete after their arrival in New Zealand in early March 1874 and clearing quarantine.

_____

Buckinghamshire

Return of Owners of Land, 1873

The results of this survey for Buckinghamshire were very similar to Oxfordshire's, with only two great estates over 10,000 acres, owned by Lord Carington of Whitehall, South West London, with 14,835 acres and Earl Brownlow of Berkhamsted, with 11,785 acres (see Table 7). However, there were two other estates only just under 10,000 acres, the Duke of Buckingham at Stowe with 9,511 acres, and Baron L.N. de Rothschild at Waddesdon with 9,959 acres. There were also three landowners with holdings in more than one county: The Duke of Bedford of Woburn Abbey, with 3,036 acres in Buckinghamshire and 3,416 acres in Northamptonshire, Lord Overtone with 5,072 acres in Buckinghamshire, 15, 045 in Overstone Park, Northamptonshire, and 4,460 acres in Warwickshire, and the Duke of Grafton at Wakefield Lodge, with 7,316 acres in Buckinghamshire and 8,458 acres in Northamptonshire. It is also interesting that Lady Dashwood of West Wycombe owned 4,888 acres, while her husband, Sir Henry, owned 7,515 acres in Kirtlington, Oxon.

Population Changes

Table 4 shows the significant decline in the populations of a selection of villages from 1851 to 1911, ranging from 22% to 48%. Most of the peaks were in 1851 or earlier. The towns grew significantly by 81% to 296%, except for Buckingham which declined by 18% from its peak in 1841, possibly because the new railways did not benefit the town. The county's population grew by 34%.

Emigration

Aylesbury Poor Law Union
Aylesbury
As noted above, Edward Richardson, the Aylesbury Agitator, sailed with a large party on the *Ramsey* from Gravesend on 28 March 1873 with 367 emigrants on board and arrived in Moreton Bay (Brisbane) on 28 June 1873. The party included emigrants from both of the Miltons and Haseleys, Worminghall, Ickford, Holton and other Oxfordshire parishes. On 13 September 1874, the *Indus* sailed from London with 586 emigrants, of which the Buckinghamshire party, sponsored and accompanied by Richardson, totalled 197. The ship arrived in Moreton Bay on 26 December 1874.

Winslow Poor Law Union
Swanbourne
In March 1873, as noted above, following a strike of agricultural labourers in Swanbourne, near Winslow, nearly all of them accepted the terms offered by Sir Thomas Fremantle. These required them to resign from the newly formed NALU, which most of them did in spite of a visit from Joseph Arch. A few of them looked at the possibility of emigration and at least three eventually went to Queensland.[lxxv]

Wycombe Poor Law Union
Radnage
17 March 1864, Rebecca Britnell, born c.1828 at Monks Risborough, (her late husband, John, farmed at Bennett End, Radnage) left with her six children, aged 14 to 2. The ship arrived in Melbourne in June 1864, after 140 days. The passage was unassisted. In 1879, her son, George, left Creswick, Victoria, and settled in New Zealand, where he lived in Wairoa.

Northamptonshire

Return of Owners of Land, 1873
The survey's figures for Northamptonshire include five estates over 10,000 acres, The Duke of Buccleuch of Whitehall, South West London, with 17,965 acres, the Marquis of Exeter of Burghley, Stamford, with 13,545 acres, the Hon. George W. Fitzwilliam of Peterborough, with 18,116 acres, Lord Overtone of Overstone Park, with 15,045 acres, and the Earl Spencer of Althorp Park, with 17,080 acres. The

Duke of Buccleuch also had 6,881 acres in Warwickshire, Sir Charles Mordaunt of Walton Hall, Warwick, 3,270 acres in Northamptonshire and 3,325 acres in Warwickshire. and the Marquis of Northampton 9,649 acres in Northamptonshire and 4,985 acres in Warwickshire. The county also had 28 landowners in the category below 10,000 acres, compared to 20-22 in the other three counties.

Population Changes

Table 5 shows the significant decline in the populations of most of the villages from 1871 or earlier, ranging from 13% to 38%. The towns of Northampton and Wellingborough both grew significantly, while Daventry and Towcester both declined, perhaps because the growth of the railways did not help them.

Emigration

The following comments about the economy in the correspondence of the Terry family of Tingewick are of interest:

1855, 'wages very low on account of the Russian war [Crimean] in part.'

1859, 'farmers have sunk their men to eighteen pence a day!'

1863-65, '3 particular good harvests.'

1867, 'old England full of trouble this last 12 months- plague among cattle which destroyed hundreds and thousands of cows, calves and grate [sic] many people died. Cholera v.bad in some parts.'

1870, 'State of this country- it still gets worse, everything v.dear in accordance with wages. A great many more out of work in every parish. Never was so many known to be out of work.'

Individual Parishes

Banbury Poor Law Union

Chipping Warden, Oxfordshire

15 May 1851, To Adelaide, Australia, embarked on the *Thetis:* John Lines, single; Thomas, single; William Lucas; John Lovell; Thomas Hawkes

Brackley Poor Law Union

Syresham

22 March 1853, Poor Law Authorisation form, from Syresham, Brackley Union, to raise £55 for emigrants.

23 March 1853, Agreement between Guardians of the Brackley Union and (? Shepherds) Thomas William and George Ford, Emigration Agents of 26 Birchin Lane, London to receive the persons on 7th April named in the Schedule, together with bedding and any luggage, on board the ship *Ava* in the Port of Southampton......and will convey them to the Port of Quebec and land them. People named: George James, 27, William James, 9, Ann, 32, Hannah, 13, Elizabeth, 10, Sarah Ann, 2. See Chapter 7 for details of costs involved.

16 April 1853, Syresham letter applying to Poor Law Commissioners, Whitehall, for the Sale of part of the Stock (now invested belonging to this Parish) to defray the expenses lately incurred in the emigration of George James and family to America. Total sum of expenses incurred in the same amounts to about forty-seven pounds.[lxxvi]

Kettering Poor Law Union
Geddington
On 12 November 1851, the Poor Law Board of Kettering authorized the Parish of Geddington to raise £15 for 'defraying the expenses of the Emigration of poor persons having settlement in the said Parish.'[lxxvii]

Pytchley
On 15 October 1852, the Poor Law Board of Kettering authorized the Parish of Pytchley to raise £12 for 'defraying the expenses of the Emigration of poor persons having settlement in the said Parish.'[lxxviii]

Pottersbury Poor Law Union
Ashton
16 Feb 1869, letter from John Simpson of Stony Stratford to the Revd A.C.Neely re payments for emigration of people of Ashton to America. He mentions Alice Tebbutt and says that he has only £50 to spend and suggests the following amounts for each adult:

'If Wm Jones go we have I believe equal to 7 and a half or 8 adults = £48. He does not wish them to be totally destitute but each should have a few shillings to begin life in America with (See also Chapter 7).[lxxix]

Warwickshire

Return of Owners of Land, 1873
This survey shows that the county had four estates over 10,000 acres, the Earl of Aylesford of Aylesford, with 12,158 acres, the Marquis of Hereford, of Ragley Hall, Alcester, with 10,281 acres, Lord Leigh of Stoneleigh Abbey with 14,981 acres, and Lord Willoughby De Broke of Compton Verney, with 12,621 acres. It is also interesting to see Sir N.W. Throckmorton of Coughton Court, with 7,618 acres, the Earl of Warwick of Warwick Castle with 8,262 acres, and Sir Robert Peel, former Prime Minister, with 3,075 acres in Tamworth (see Table 7). .

Population Changes
Table 6 shows the decline in the population of a sample of villages in Warwickshire, most of them in excess of 20% and up to 53%. The peak

populations were mostly prior to 1871. From 1851 to 1911, there was growth in all the selected towns, by 8% up to 123%, and in the county as a whole by 119%.

Emigration

General Information
In August 1857, The Australian Land & Emigration Co Ltd, Application for Shares: Land will be sold in blocks of 40 acres. List of current wages at Sydney: Town rates of pay most 10.0 -14.0 up to 15/6. Annual rate for ag.lab. plus rations £30, plus wife £50.

Individual Parishes

Banbury Poor Law Union
Ratley, Warwickshire
4 Nov 1852, to Sydney, Australia: Thomas Barnes, 30, Mary, 29, and 3 children and Richard Webb Harrison, 9 (illegitimate son of Mary Barnes); William Grimston, 30, Elizabeth, 29, Sarah Ann, 1.

19 Nov 1852, to Victoria, Australia: Elizabeth, 45, wife of transported labourer, seamstress, Hannah, 24, single, Thomas, 22, single, William Richard, 14.

1852, James Gibbs, sentenced to seven years Transportation, now at Liberty (Term of transportation having expired), resident in the Colony of Victoria, has sent £30 to enable his wife and children under 10, to join him.

2 Feb 1853, to Australia: George Grant, 27, Catherine, 24, Elizabeth, 2, Fanny, 4 months.

Shotteswell, Warwockshire
9 Sep 1852, to Sydney, Australia: William Purser, 26, Charlotte, 25, Elizabeth, 4, Eliza, 3, Dara, 1.

Rugby Poor Law Union
Cubbington
It is interesting that the population of Cubbington grew from 885 in 1851 to 1,164 by 1901, by 31%. The village was close to Leamington and part of the growing industrial north of the county and not like the pastoral south.

Annie Saunders (née Shaylor) was born in 1869 at Cubbington, a few miles from Leamington, where she trained as a nurse at the Warneford Hospital and graduated in 1885. She married Frederick Saunders in 1890 and had two boys. In 1906 she emigrated to Canada, arriving in Halifax on 29 March and then taking another 8 days to reach the mining district of Cobalt in Northern Ontario. She was appointed as the administrator of a new hospital there built by the mine owners. After spending many years there and elsewhere in North America, she finally returned to Cubbington, where she died in 1932, aged 64.[lxxx] (see further details in Chapter 8).

Leamington
30 June 1853, John Addinsall, agricultural labourer, 38, with his wife, Mary, 30, and 4 children, age 1-10, boarded the *Oithona* at Southampton on her maiden voyage to Port Phillip (Melbourne). The ship anchored at Portland on 2 October 1853 but as there was no work there, they continued on to Port Fairy (name changed to Belfast on 1 January 1854 but later changed back). The couple were both natives of Lincoln but had moved to Leamington; they were Wesleyans and able to read and write. On arrival in Port Philip, John was engaged to work for H.Gardiner of Belfast, for 50 shillings per week, without rations. In 1855, he bought land from his brother-in-law, Richard Burgin, in Muddy Creek, 5 miles west of The Grange (Hamilton). In 1856, he and his family walked from Port Fairy to Muddy Creek, a distance of 90 kilometres (60 miles).[lxxxi]

Shipston-on-Stour Poor Law Union
Tysoe
In 1877, Joseph Ashby's Uncle William emigrated to the States, leaving for ever his wife and a large family of young children. 'His departure turned many a mind to emigration.' After 1877, the exodus became slower but did not cease but went by twos and threes after the great exodus. 'Emigrants letters spoke of 'free-growing fruits' in Vermont, the 'land of liberty', the States, where every man can speak his thoughts, of Australia's plentiful meat. Sometimes the men in Australia would comment on the wasteful, unskilled farmwork they saw - it wanted more of the Tysoe men!'[lxxxii]

Chapter 7

Migrant Ports, Shipping and Passages

Migrant Ports

a. Liverpool

Liverpool had been the centre of the slave trade until its abolition in 1807 but the port developed a new role in the transportation of emigrants after the end of the French wars in 1815. In 1818, a regular scheduled packet boat service was started to New York, originally intended for business travel and freight. Emigrants were attracted to it from throughout the British Isles and after 1830 Liverpool was the most popular emigrant port in Europe. In 1830 some 15,000 sailed from it and by 1842 this had risen to 200,000, more than half of all emigrants from Europe. By 1845, 20,521 ships were trading through the port, and by then Liverpool had a fine new Customs House, built by John Foster from 1828-39. In 1851, Liverpool sent approximately 160,000 passengers to North America alone. It was cheaper for most travellers from Northern Europe, to take ship to Hull and then make their way across to Liverpool by train to board a ship for America. During the period 1830 to 1930 over 9 million emigrants left Liverpool in search of a new life in the United States, Canada and Australia.[lxxxiv] Liverpool also began regular voyages to Australia and New Zealand, though, by 1860, these destinations proved popular from other UK ports, particularly London and Southampton and, to a lesser extent, Plymouth and Bristol.

Interestingly, Francis Kilvert (1840-79), the noted diarist, made a trip to Liverpool in June 1872. He was enormously impressed with the Exchange building 'one of the finest buildings of its kind in the world'. From the gallery, 'we looked down upon a crowd of merchants and brokers swarming and humming like a hive of bees in the floor of the vast area below.' 'The Mersey was gay and almost crowded with vessels of all sorts moving up and down the river, ships, barques, brigs, brigantines, schooners, cutters, colliers, tugs, steamboats, lighters, 'flats', everything from the huge emigrant liner steamship with four masts to the tiny sailing and rowing boat. From the river one sees to advantage the miles of docks which line the Mersey side, and the forests of masts which crowd the quays, 'the pine forest of the sea, mast and spar'. No wonder many of the expectant emigrants were overwhelmed by the experience.

'As we came down the river this morning several large emigrant ships lay in the river getting up steam and the Blue Peter, the signal for sailing, flying at the fore. They were going down the river this afternoon. They seemed crowded with Irish and German emigrants and small steam-boats kept bringing fresh loads of passengers alongside the big ships. One could not help thinking of the hundreds of sorrowful hearts on board and ashore and the farewells and partings forever, so many of them, on this side of the grave.'

He visited the Docks later and 'Nothing gives one so vivid an idea of the vast commerce of the country as these docks, quays and immense warehouses, piled and cumbered with hides, cotton, tallow, corn, oil-cake, wood and wine, oranges and other fruit and merchandise of all kinds from all corners of the world.' His hostess also said that 15, 10 and even 5 years ago there was much more trade and wealth in Liverpool and much larger fortunes more rapidly made than now. There has been of late and there still is a stagnation of trade, a depression and deterioration of credit. Formerly the streets were blocked by enormous business and the mountains of merchandise passing about, but there is plenty of room now.' Liverpool left Kilvert 'with an impression of ragged Irish bare-footed women and children. enormous wealth and squalid poverty, wildernesses of offices and palatial counting houses and warehouses, bustling pushing vulgar men, pretty women and lovely children.'[lxxxv]

This contemporary view of Liverpool in the 1870s serves as confirmation that by the late nineteenth century, Liverpool's dominant role was being challenged - particularly by German ports, such as Bremen and Hamburg, but also by Southampton. By then emigrants increasingly came from the countries of southern and eastern Europe. Liverpool built a very fine Customs House to handle all these emigrants and there was a public uproar in 1948, when it was pulled down to make way for the new Albert Dock. In the early twentieth century the 'Three Graces' were built: the Port Authority (1907), the Liver (1911) and the Cunard (1916) Buildings. They are all superb, grand and impressive. In 1926, however, Liverpool's position was further weakened when the United States imposed restrictions on immigration.

We have seen a number of examples of local parties of emigrants being guided to Liverpool, a journey of some eight days in wagons and on foot, such as the 1830 party from King's Sutton. These parties largely consisted of agricultural labourers with little education and no experience of travel. They would also never have seen or experienced a large bustling city like Liverpool which would have left them very confused and frightened. Most of them spent between one and ten days waiting for their ship in a lodging house. In the 1840s and 1850s, these were often inhospitable, dirty and overcrowded. The city was also full of colonial and emigration agents, with a variety of offers of accommodation and ships. There were also numerous suppliers of all necessities for the passage, which exposed emigrants to all sorts of pressures to buy them. In the mid-19th century, emigrants

Canning Dock and the Customs House, Liverpool, 1860s (Liverpool City Council).

Liverpool from the Pier Head, c.1906 (Liverpool City Council).

The "Three Graces", Liverpool, 1920s (Liverpool City Council).

'1913 Setting Sail for a Better life a World Away.': Tender 'Herald' leaves Liverpool for the 'Zealandic' bound for Australia (Liverpool City Council).

were also liable to harassment and fraud by local confidence tricksters, who became known as 'runners'. Runners frequently snatched the emigrants' luggage and would only return it if the emigrant paid a large fee.

From the 1860s the situation began to improve as steam started to replace sail, and the steamship companies started to look after emigrants during their stay in Liverpool, with their representatives meeting the emigrants on arrival in the city. The emigrants were taken to lodging houses which were frequently owned by the steamship companies, but delays still occurred and there continued to be complaints about treatment in Liverpool even in the early 20th century. One positive sign was the treatment of Jewish emigrants in 1882, when some 600 per week were arriving in Liverpool from Europe on their way to the United States. They were helped by the Liverpool Anglo-Jewish Committee.

There were some particular Fringford connections with Liverpool, involving two of the Butler family and George Whitton, son of Kezia and John Whitton who ran the forge and Post Office where Flora Thompson, author of *Lark Rise to Candleford*, worked in the 1890s. Joseph and Henry Butler both moved to Liverpool to work for the railway prior to emigrating to Northern Queensland in 1869-70. George Whitton moved to Liverpool and worked for the HM Customs Service, initially in 1881 as a clerk. By 1891, he was a Stationery Officer, and the same in 1901. By 1911 he was a Surveyor of the Customs Service. He moved house three times and educated his children privately at the Merchant Taylors School in Crosby, near Liverpool, which shows what a successful career could be had in the Customs Service.[lxxxvi]

b. Other Ports

By 1860, regular voyages from other UK ports had become popular, notably London (Gravesend) and Southampton and to a lesser extent Plymouth and Bristol. The south coast ports were more convenient for emigrants coming from mainland Europe, particularly from Hamburg, on their way to the USA or one of the British colonies. There was also significant emigration from Cornwall and Devon, mainly of out-of-work miners, for whom the ports of Liverpool and London necessitated a long journey, certainly before the railways. Ports on the north and south coasts of Cornwall and Devon were therefore important points of departure, including Padstow, Fowey, Truro, Falmouth, Penzance and St Ives, together with Plymouth and Bideford. A great many of these Cornish emigrants went to Canada and the USA between 1831 and 1860. From Padstow alone, some 6,200 emigrants sailed to Canada in those years. Indeed in 1841, Padstow was the third most important departure point for Canada, surpassed only by Liverpool and London. (See Appendix 3 for further information on Cornish emigration).

Costs

The following are examples of the costs involved in some of the emigration cases noted above:

1. 1829, the Dorchester overseers spent £29 17s in sending 2 men to America, the passage costing £17. In 1832, a family of 7 emigrated at a cost to the parish of £30.

2. 1830, a party from King's Sutton was conveyed by wagons at a cost of £20 but the group included a number of persons from another parish for which King's Sutton was reimbursed £5. The journey to Liverpool took eight days. The total expenses was £206.18s.3d, of which £11.16s.7½ was still due. They lodged 'at Mr John BROWNS nr Princes Dock.' The cost of accommodation in Liverpool was 7s for adults, 4s for children. The records also include details of the cost of provisions for a man, wife and 6 children, and of the provisions purchased. The supplier was James Beckett, possibly the same or an associate of Donovan & Beckets mentioned as brokers for the voyage from Liverpool.[lxxxvii]

3. 1835, Stanton St John: Passage from Liverpool to Quebec about £3.3s., a little more or less; passengers paid for their own provisions. To New York about £3.10s. Children under 14 half price. Provisions about 40/- each. Hospital money 4/6 for each man, woman and child. Taking passenger to Liverpool: 14/- for grown persons, 7/- for children and 4/6 for luggage.

4. 1837, Articles required - on fitting out a person - a labourer - for the Cape from Captain Wolfe:

    24 Shirts altogether those now purchased by him 'Check'
    2 Suits of Russia (possibly russet ting, a dull brownish red material)
        Jackets Waistcoats and trousers
    12 Cotton Flannel kerchiefs
    2 pairs of good shoes
    1 Forage cap to wear on board ship
    12 pair socks
    6 lbs of ?dense (so unrefined) soap
    2 lbs Tobacco

    Mattress, Pillows, Blankets and Counterpane-all of a Common Sort with a Common Sailors Cot

    The above for one Man with a chest with a good Lock and Key.

    Any fitting out shop will complete the order, say Kiplings in the Strand.[lxxxix]

5. 18 Aug 1838, Pytchley: Letter from Rev'd A.W.Brown re Application for Free Passage to South Australia of the Flavel and Dainty families. Passage for 9 children to be paid by a parish officer (9x £3 = £27), all necessary comforts provided before they go on board, expenses to London and other expenses.

List given: Waggon charge £3.0.0, Mrs Flavel £10, Bread & cheese & beer £5 and Mr Laurenson £5.0.0, Expenses: Shoes £5.10, Bedding for 2 families £8.10.3, Tools £3.14.3, Clothing £13.16.8, pocket money £2.10 = £34.5.2. Clothing included: Smocks, trousers, caps, stockings, frocks, girls ? and 10 yds flannel.[lxxxix]

6. 15 Feb 1844, Memo of Great Linford Parish meeting on assisted emigration with names and calculations. It was considered that about £200 must be raised for such purpose and it was decided that a 4 penny rate should be raised amongst the Occupiers of land which would amount to about £40 plus such a rate upon the land owners would amount to about £160 = £200. It seems to show costs per adult as follows: Passage to Montreal £6.15, Clothing £1.10, Landing money £1.0 & 9s 6d, Shoes 13s - Total £10.7.6. Someone wishes to board himself requires £20 to New York.[xc]

7. 12 March 1844, Expenses of the Faulkners and party from Pytchley to Melbourne to embark in London. Very detailed summary of the expenses, amounting to £55.9.8, of which £1.4.0 was unpaid. It also discloses how the money was raised: An Owners rate of 2d on land not tithe £26.6.5, and an Occupiers rate of 2d on land £30.7.31 = £56.13.8½.[xci]

8. 30 July 1850, Pytchley: Final list of expenses for the emigration of 35 persons - on the *Posthumous*, 20 May, the *Lysander*, 30 May, and the *Constance*, 2 July,- to Adelaide, South Australia. Passage Fares- £228.4.3. Total- £366.7.4. Families unable to pay off all, because of want of work and high prices of 1847. Some possessions sold but no real value.[xcii]

9. 23 March 1853, Syresham: under the Agreement between Guardians of the Brackley Union and (?) Shepherds, Thomas William and George Ford, Emigration Agents, they will convey the James family of six to the Port of Quebec on the *Ava*. Money paid by Syresham: Steerage £23, Landing Money £4, Other expenses £19.17.0, Total £46.17.0.[xciii]

10. 16 February 1869, letter from John Simpson to the Revd A.C.Neely re payments for emigration to America from Ashton, Northamptonshire. He expects 8 people at £8 each as follows: £4 10.0, Expenses to London 10.0, A few extra days 10.0, Pocket money (say) 10.0 = £6.0.0. He has my £50 to spend but he does not want them to be totally destitute but each should have a few shillings to buy a life in America with.[xciv]

11. 1887, Bloxham: £2 was paid to a man to go to Droitwich, £6 2s 6d to help a man emigrate to Canada and £10 to a family for the same purpose.

Shipping

The 19th and early 20th centuries were the great age of passenger travel at sea, and with the development of sea transport came a massive expansion of emigration. America was the primary destination, with many seeking to escape war, poverty and religious and political persecution in search of a better life. Canada and Australia also attracted millions. The dream of the emigrant was to arrive in a country where he was told that land was free and fertile, religious and political dissent was tolerated, and class division did not exist, or what you might call 'The Promised Land'. During the period 1850 to 1914, some 13 million emigrated from the UK.

Initially, the shipping companies were more interested in transporting mail and merchandise than in carrying passengers. However, it was soon realized that good passenger facilities brought status and increasing custom and large liners were built to transport emigrants, with first-class conditions on the upper decks for the wealthy, and 'steerage', with communal cooking and living arrangements on the lower decks, for the poor. The main shipping companies in Liverpool, Cunard (1839), White Star (1845), Inman (1850) and the Liverpool and Great Western Steamship Company (Guion) (1866), were quick to involve themselves in the emigrant trade once they realized that this could be lucrative. The 1855 Passenger Act also helped to improve conditions, laying down minimum standards for rations, space and sanitation.[xcv] In the 1830s, the run to Australia was normally between 4 and 5 months but in 1837 Brunel's *Great Western* reduced the Atlantic crossing to 15 days. In the 1860s, 75 or 80 days became a realistic target for the Australian run and steamships started to replace sailing ships, cutting the length of the journey time to North America from over four weeks to about eight days, and to Australia from 10-17 weeks to 4-6 weeks. In 1868, the Suez Canal opened, which cut 1,000 miles off the Australia run. In 1907, the White Star Line moved the focus of its operations to Southampton, which since 1858 had been used by British shipping companies and their major continental rivals. By 1870, virtually all emigrants went by steamship. Competition between the steamship companies helped to improve conditions for the emigrants. From about 1900, third-class cabins began to replace the steerage accommodation. Accommodation was still Spartan but it was a considerable improvement.

In Britain there had long been depots for emigrants on government assisted passages to Australia and New Zealand. Facilities in them were basic but made a good impression on agents for the colonies and medical inspectors. In 1883, for example, the assistant Agent-General for South Australia, impressed by the cleanliness of the beds and walls at the Plymouth Emigrant Depot, 'had no idea that emigrants were so well treated.' In 1879, John Hillary and his family found the same depot relatively clean, but thought that many of the emigrants there

Table 8
Emigrant Ships used by the Four Shires, 1823-1912 (Note 1)

Date	Ship Name	Emigrant/Parish	From	To	Arrived
17 May 1823	Mariner	M.Steel, Begbroke		Hobart	26-Sep-23
11 June 1827	Prince Regent	Stoke Lyne	Deal	Sydney	27-Sep-27
May 1830	Warren	Bicester group	Liverpool	USA	
1832	Forth	Tingewick		Stanley,VDL	
2 December 1839	Morley	Pytchley	Liverpool	Adelaide	
12 December 1839	Eliza	Pytchley	Liverpool	Adelaide	
20 December 1841	Clifford	Blincoe/Windsor		Nelson, NZ	
3 November 1843	Wallace	Aston Rowant		Pt Phillip	16-Feb-44
26 March 1845	Canton	Eydon	Liverpool	Canada	
20 April 1845	Cataraqui	Tackley et al	Liverpool	Pt Phillip	**Note2**
10 May 1845	William Braham	Eydon	Liverpool	Canada	
17 May 1845	St Ann's	S.Newington	Liverpool	Canada	
29 May 1845	Royal Albert	Adderbury	Liverpool	Canada	
29 March 1848	Mahomed Shah	Chilterns		Pt Phillip	5 July/48
March 1848	Palmyra	Twyford		Pt Phillip	Jul-48
14 July 1848	Emperor	Twyford	Plymouth	Sydney	04-Nov-48
June 1849	Victoria	Hook Norton	Liverpool	Canada	
1850	Statesman	Chilterns		Pt Phillip	17 Mar/50
20 May 1850	Posthumous	Pytchley	Liverpool	Adelaide	
30 May 1850	Lysander	Pytchley	Liverpool	Adelaide	
2 July 1850	Constance	Pytchley	Liverpool	Adelaide	
28 May 1851	Sisters	Wroxton	Liverpool	Canada	
15 May 1851	Thetis	Chipping Warden	Liverpool	Adelaide	
28 May 1851	Sisters	Wroxton	Liverpool	Canada	
7 April 1853	Ava	Syresham	S'hampton	Quebec	
25 April 1853	Thomas Harrison	Alfred Joy, Oxford	Graves'nd	Melbourne	22Sep/53
30 June 1853	Oithona	Leamington	S'hampton	Pt Phillip	
17 March 1864	Red Rose	Radnage		Melbourne	June/64
9 December 1869	Royal Dane	Butler/Fringford	Graves'nd	Rockhampton	
30 July 1870	Royal Dane	Butler/Fringford	Gravesn'd	Rockhmpt'n19Nov/70	
13 Sep 1872		Wychwoods		Hawkes Bay28Dec/72	
28 March 1873	Ramsey	Aylesbury group	Graves'nd	Moret'n Bay28Jun/73	
23 December 1873	Mongol	Wootton	Plymouth	Dunedin,NZ Mar/74	
24 December 1873	Scimitar	Wootton	Plymouth	Dunedin,NZ Mar/74	
December 1873	Inverene	Wychwoods		Hawkes Bay, NZ	
28 February 1874	Ballochmyle	Oxon group	Plymouth	Canterbury, NZ	
10 April 1874	Stonehouse	Islip	Plymouth	Christchurch,NZ	
29 May 1874	Zoroaster	Oxon & Bucks	Graves'nd	Moreton Bay	
24 June 1874	Cartvale	Butler,Fritwell	Blackwall	Wellington, NZ	
25 July 1874	Darling Downs	Butler/Fringford	London	Brisbane	05-Nov-74
11 September 1874	Cospatrick	Wychwood	London	Auckland,NZ **Note3**	
13 September 1874	Indus	Aylesbury group	London	Brisbane	26-Dec-74
1878	Hankow	Banbury		Melbourne	
1912 January	Demosthenes	Juniper Hill	London	Sydney	

Notes

1. These ships were noted during my research.

2. The Cataraqui was wrecked on 4 August 1845.

3. The Cospatrick was destroyed by fire on 17 November 1874.

'Darling Downs', Gravesend Reach, River Thames, 1852 (National Maritime Museum).

'Cospatrick', built 1856, Gravesend Reach, River Thames) (National Maritime Museum).

Ramsay, Gravesend Reach, River Thames, 1863 (National Maritime Museum).

Victoria, entering New York Harbour (Liverpool City Council).

Constance, Australian Clipper Ship, built 1848, (Liverpool City Council).

Hankow, passenger/cargo liner, Gravesend Reach, River Thames, 1873
(National Maritime Museum).

Demosthenes, passenger/cargo liner, Gravesend Reach, River Thames, 1911
(National Maritime Museum).

R.M.S. Titanic, , which foundered on her Maiden Voyage to New York,
April 15th, 1912. (Liverpool City Council).

Sydney Harbour in late-19th century, end of a long journey
(National Maritime Museum).

were dirty and diseased. They were disturbed by having to mix with people 'of the lowest type', and later suspected that it was mixing with a lower class of person that resulted in their children falling sick on the voyage, and the whole family being quarantined when they arrived in New Zealand.

At Liverpool, Cunard began to provide free accommodation for emigrants awaiting embarkation in what amounted to 'a village by itself in the centre of Liverpool, and consists of several buildings, holding over 2,000 guests if need be'.[xcvi] Guests were greeted on arrival by a matron and hotel keeper in Cunard uniform, who offered refreshments and showed guests to their quarters. Men and women were strictly segregated and accommodated in dormitories sleeping no more than fifteen people, which were 'well-ventilated and provided with heat and electric light.' Wholesome food was offered in the dining rooms. The 'Cunard Hotel system' was visited daily by a company doctor to carry out medical examinations to identify any ill or diseased passengers who might be rejected on reaching America.

This system was certainly superior to that of the average emigrant depots. But there were attempts to reassure people both at home and in the colonies that emigrants, especially young women, passing through depots were well looked after. In 1883, Ellen Joyce, as a supporter of female emigration, was impressed by the services held for young women going to Queensland by the sub-matron of the Plymouth Depot, and the singing of an appropriate hymn, 'Go Forward Christian Emigrant Beneath His Banner True'. As a group, they had been allowed to form their own mess [separate party for taking meals] and choose a mess captain from amongst themselves. Medical inspections, 'passing the doctor', had been suitably decorous. Mrs Joyce was keen to reassure families of the young women that they would be well looked after, physically, morally and spiritually.[xcvii]

Emigrant Paintings

The scene as the emigrant ship set sail is vividly evoked by the artist Henry O'Neil in his 1861 painting *The Parting Cheer.* and by Charles Staniland in his painting *The Emigrant Ship* in the late 1880s. Both the artists concentrated on the emotions of those left behind as an emigrant ship leaves from an undefined location. There was a real sense of excitement when a ship set sail, mingled with apprehension and a great deal of confusion. In December 1850, for example, when the *Star of the West* set sail down the River Mersey 'the spectators on shore took off their hats and cheered lustily, and the cheer was repeated by the whole body of emigrants on deck, who raised a shout that must have been heard at the distance of a mile even in the noisy and busy thoroughfares of Liverpool'. There was no going back at this point and the passage to a new life had begun.

There were three famous Victorian emigrant paintings:

1. In 1852, Ford Madox Brown painted *The Last of England*, in which, as models, he chose himself, his wife and children and selected another from 'all the red-headed boys in Finchley'. It was inspired by the departure of his friend, Thomas Woolner, for Australia in July 1852 in search of gold. After he had finished it, he wrote 'The picture is in the strictest sense historical. It treats of the great emigration movement. The educated are bound to their country by quite other ties than the illiterate man, whose chief consideration is food and physical comfort. I have therefore in order to present the parting scene in its fullest tragic development, singled out a couple from the middle classes, high enough through education and refinement to appreciate all that they are now giving up and yet depressed enough in means to have to put up with the discomforts and humiliations incident to a vessel "all one class".'

2. In 1861, Henry Nelson O'Neil painted *The Parting Cheer*, which is the key mid-nineteenth century image addressing emigration. It focuses on the reactions of those left on shore as a ship departs, who are a mix of genders and social classes. The image reflects the rigidity of the class system, but with middle and working classes united in a display of grief. The mid-Victorian audiences would have identified social types, recognizing differences in the detailed costumes and the range of responses. The scene is set along the Thames, which is shown as an industrial landscape, with smoking chimneys and a forest of ships' masts. Such alienating effects of modernity underscore the historical reasons for mass migration. The *Saturday Review* (11 May 1861) wrote of the

The Emigrant Ship by Charles Joseph Staniland (1838-1916), late-1880s (Bradford Art Galleries and Museums/Bridgeman Images).

Emigrants at dinner below deck on a migration ship, the Illustrated London News, 13 April 1844 (National Maritime Museum)..

painting that: 'never, perhaps, do Englishmen throw off their reserve as on the occasion of such a parting, and we doubt whether the varied forms of demonstrative grief here expressed are at all exaggerated'.

3. In the late 1880s, Charles Joseph Staniland, the Yorkshire artist, painted *The Emigrant Ship*, which focuses on the people who stand at the dock to watch

their loved ones go. All social classes are represented and all have a story to tell. The overall impression from the scene is of expectant excitement on board, mingled with bafflement and sorrow onshore at the loss of loved ones to lands far from England. The agricultural clothes of the old man, woman and child at the centre of the painting, and the sheepdog, suggests that a young man, probably a son, from a village was leaving in search of work overseas.

Passages

These three paintings reveal the wide range of interest in the great emigration movement.They also show the mix of classes and the range of emotions involved. Between 1860-1900, an estimated 1.5 million farm workers emigrated from Britain and most of them found a better standard of living, and a less divided society. There must have been an element of excitement among those headed for (say) America or Australia but also some nervousness about the dangers of the voyage. The length of the journeys and the conditions on board were improving by the 1850s but more needed to be done. For those on shore, there was sorrow at the real possibility of never seeing your son and his family again.

But these stirring send-offs were only a prelude to the real horrors of steerage, with hundreds of people crowded together in squalid, cramped, poorly-lit compartments for journeys that could take about six weeks to North America in the days of sail, or up to 17 weeks to Australia, and considerably longer with adverse winds and bad weather. In 1853-54, as noted above, Alfred Joy's passage to Melbourne took 155 'tedious' days. After 1837, steamers started to challenge sail, once Brunel's paddle steamer *Great Western* reduced the advertised time of the Atlantic crossing to 15 days. After the mid 1850s, a new non-stop route to Australia picked up the Roaring Forties for a high-speed dash across the Southern Ocean. By then many sailing ships also had auxiliary steam engines powered by a single screw, so that they did not get becalmed in the doldrums and made 75-80 days a realistic target. By the 1870s, steamships were regularly carrying emigrants to Australia, although sailing ships continued to the end of the 19th century. Improved engines allowed ships to maintain speeds of 15 knots, cutting the journey down to six weeks.

Disasters

In 1847-52, only 43 emigrant ships were lost out of the 6,877 which left British ports, and out of 1,421,704 passengers on them, only 1,043 died as a result of shipwreck or fire.[xcviii] Many fell victim to the epidemics rife on the emigrant ships, which were the true killers. These were some of the major disasters in the period:

Burning of the emigrant ship Ocean Monarch, 24 Aug 1848, possibly by Prince de Joinville (National Maritime Museum).

1. In 1834, 17 sailing ships were lost in the Gulf of St Lawrence and 731 emigrants were drowned.[xcix]

2. On 4 August 1845, as noted above, the wreck of the *Cataraqui* occurred off King Island, Australia's worst maritime disaster, just one day short of their destination in Port Phillip. The ship sunk and broke up, leaving 399 dead and only 9 survivors (8 of them crewmen). Fortunately, David Howie, who was on the Island collecting animal furs, was able to help the survivors. They were eventually picked up and delivered to Melbourne on 13 September. On 2 August 2020, to mark the 175th anniversary of the shipwreck, a cairn with a ship's bell and a plaque listing all the names of the dead, was unveiled on King Island by Greta Robinson, great granddaughter of David Howie. There is a beautifully carved oak door in St Nicholas Church, Tackley, dedicated to the 42 villagers who died in the shipwreck.[c]

3. In April 1847, the *Exmouth* sailing from Londonderry to Quebec, ran aground on rocks off Islay; only 3 crew survived and about 240 emigrants perished.[ci]

4. In August 1848, the *Ocean Monarch* caught fire shortly after leaving Liverpool for Boston. 176 of the 360 on board died (see painting).[cii]

5. 23 January 1856, the *Pacific* emigrant paddle steamer sailed from Liverpool for New York with almost 200 passengers and crew. One of the largest, fastest and most well-appointed ships of her day, she vanished. Her skipper, Captain Eldridge, was renowned and two years before, sailing the *Red Jacket*, had made the crossing in 13 days and one hour. This record has never been broken and Red Jacket is one of the seven fastest sailing ships in history. The search revealed no trace of the *Pacific* or her 45 passengers and 141 crew. But a chance discovery by divers in 1991 located the bow section of the ship a few miles off

The *Cataraqui* cairn, with a ship's bell and plaque, unveiled on King Island, Australia,
on 2 August 2020 to mark the 175th anniversary of the shipwreck
(Tackley Local History Group)..

Anglesey – only about 60 miles from Liverpool. The most likely explanation is a catastrophic accident, such as a boiler explosion, that made the ship sink like a stone.[ciii]

6. In August 1858, the steamship *Austria* saw the worst fire disaster of Atlantic crossings, when a bucket of hot pine tar used for fumigation was accidentally knocked over, 471 died.

7. In October 1859, the *Royal Charter*, one of the fastest and most famous emigrant ships during the years of the Australian Gold Rush. was on the last leg of her two month journey from Melbourne, carrying 452 passengers and crew, and a cargo of gold valued at £320,000. Unfortunately she sailed into the worst storm that had hit the Irish Sea that century. In the early hours of 26 October the ship was forced on to rocks, near Moelfre Bay, only fifty yards from the shore, and broken into two pieces. One seaman, Joseph Rogers, tied a rope round his waist and managed to swim to shore. He secured the rope and aided the rescue of the 39 survivors – all men. A memorial was placed on the cliff top, reading: 'Where the *Royal Charter* met its end and the memory of those who died.'[civ]

8. In April 1873, the *Atlantic* hit Meagher's Rock on the coast of Nova Scotia, 546 of 862 on board died.[cv]
9. On 17 November 1874, as mentioned above, the *Cospatrick* caught fire 250 miles west of the Cape of Good Hope, on its way to Auckland. Only three members survived out of 470 on board. Seven Wychwood residents were lost, all members of the families of Richard Hedges and Henry Townsend. Four years later a stone memorial fountain was erected on the Green at Shipton-under-Wychwood to commemorate the community's tragic loss.
10. On 17 March 1891, the *Utopia* collided with the *HMS Anson* in Gibraltar Bay, 564 of the 880 on board died.[cvi]

Epidemic Diseases

It was the epidemic diseases which were the real killers. Between 1845 and 1851, over 1.25 million Irish emigrated to the USA as a result of the Potato Famine. In 1847, there was a huge number of Irish deaths, some 7,000 on the crossing to North America from England and a further 10,000 died in hospitals and quarantine stations at the end of their voyage. Some 5,424 of those who died from disease, mainly cholera, are commemorated at Grosse Ile in the Gulf of St Lawrence. In the same year, the *Virginius* from Liverpool to Canada lost 158 of its 476 passengers during the voyage. Of the survivors, 106 were unloaded at the Quarantine (Q) station of Grosse Ile, suffering from typhus (in an awful state). In 1848, of those who left England for Quebec, 5,293 died of typhus during the voyage, and a further 10,037 in Canadian hospitals. Many were fleeing the famine or the Scottish Highland clearances.[cvi] In 1852, the *Ticonderogo* was equally scandalous, sailing from Liverpool to Melbourne with 795 emigrants, of whom 100 died of typhus, and an equal number of cases of the fever were still suffering when the ship went into quarantine at Port Phillip Heads. A quarantine ship was sent alongside with stores for three months. The citizens of Melbourne were appalled.[cvii]

Cholera was even more malignant and inspired greater fear. In 1853, for example, of the 77 ships that set sail from Liverpool for New York, 46 were stricken with cholera and 1,328 emigrants died of it. In 1885, the *Dorunda* carried cholera to Australia. It left London on 20 October with 290 passengers, bound for Brisbane, calling at Malta, Port Said, Aden and Batavia [now Jakarta], where cholera was endemic. Cases developed immediately and the ship sought refuge in Townsville. However, the Q station was not equipped to deal with such a serious epidemic and the ship was sent on to Moreton Bay and the Q station on Peel Island. There were 17 deaths and at least 50 cases of cholera, all confined to steerage passengers.[cviii]

Despite all the problems facing the emigrant to Australia and New Zealand, the regulatory framework of assisted passages meant a higher chance of survival than on the shorter, unregulated crossing to North America. Many Q stations began as ad hoc solutions, as at Manly at Spring Cove in Sydney Harbour, which opened in 1828 in response to the increase in the number of emigrant ships to NSW. But Queensland did not quarantine any ships until 1862, when it established a Q station on the island of St Helena in Moreton Bay. New Zealand was also relatively late in establishing Q stations, only designating Somes Island, or Matiu, in 1869. Even then it was not used as such until 1872.[cix]

If there were no health issues, passengers had few problems in landing. In November 1874, for example, for Joseph Sams on the *Northumberland* at Melbourne 'medical officer only stayed about 10 minutes and we were allowed to go with a free pass.' The ship continued to Sandridge Pier where Sams 'then wishes the ship a goodbye as far as inhabiting her went, and entered the great and prosperous city of Melbourne.'[cx] But ships could face 40 days of quarantine e.g. John Hillary on the clipper *Westland* from Plymouth to Lyttelton, South Island, New Zealand, after 86 days sailing he arrived but was quarantined with his family at the Q station on Ripa Island, opposite Lyttelton, for a month before completing his journey to Canterbury. At least he found life better there than at the Government Depot in Plymouth, 'a den of disease' and 'we can fish, bathe and enjoy ourselves'.[cxi]

It was easier for people arriving in Australia than the United States. Unlike the United States, Canada, Australia and Argentina continued to operate liberal immigration policies and to encourage immigration with assisted passages well into the 1930s. The 1852 Passenger Act allowed emigrants to stay on board free of charge for 48 hours after arrival, which gave them more time to find somewhere decent to live and even a chance to find a job. There were also immigrant depots at Melbourne, Sydney and Port Phillip where they could stay free of charge. Often all the emigrants had been engaged within 48 hours after the inspection was over. There was a scramble for housemaids, because of the scarcity of servants, the result of most young eligible women finding husbands quickly. Young females were warned against marrying the first settler they met. One young woman from Newcastle on arrival in Port Phillip was more sensible and turned down an offer of marriage with the comment 'Nay, nay hinney' she said very cavalierly, 'nay, my hinney, I'se to wait a wee and see what turns up.'[cxii]

Improvements in Health
a. The shorter length of voyages and the improvement of conditions on the ships themselves, as steamships replaced sailing ships, and standards of hygiene aboard improved, meant that outbreaks could be contained.

b. Some of the improvement was down to technological advances such as water purification and waste removal. However, the deadly typhus and cholera epidemics of the mid-19th century had focused attention on the need to reform conditions in steerage.

c. Governments responded with greater regulation of emigrant traffic, although they were reluctant to burden ship-owners and discourage emigration. By the mid-19th century, every European maritime nation and every country receiving emigrants had built up an elaborate code of regulations., covering: limited numbers to be carried, specified amount of food and water to be carried and issued and minimum standards of ventilation and sanitation.

Chapter 8

Diaries and Other Records of Emigrants

a. Michael Steel – from Begbroke, Oxfordshire to Van Diemens Land, 1823

In 1823, Michael Steel (at his own expense) emigrated from Begbroke to Van Diemen's Land (VDL) with his sister, Jane, and two servants. They sailed on the *Mariner* on 17 May, carrying merchandise and 57 passengers, and arrived in Hobart on 26 September. Steel brought with him 'implements of husbandry etc' to the value of £290 and 10,000 Spanish dollars, which led to him being called 'Dollar Steel'. This enabled him to receive a grant of 2000 acres in the Macquarrie District on the Lower Clyde River on the west coast. A number of Steel's other land deals have emerged from the Tasmanian Archives, including applications for allotments in New Norfolk (1827) and Hamilton (1831), at both of which he committed to erect a good brick building with seven or eight rooms, and a grant of 189 acres in Melville (1847). These land deals enabled him to become a very wealthy man.

His brother, William, also emigrated to VDL in 1829 and settled in Falmouth. By 1832, he had built a home 'Thomsons Villa', later called 'Enstone Park'. He decided to build a flour mill and sent to England for the machinery. It arrived in 1834 and he went to Hobart to join the ship for the journey up the east coast. He insisted on coming into Georges Bay rather than Falmouth. Sadly, while the dinghy was coming over the bar-way a big wave capsized it and William was drowned along with the Captain and a Mr Dunn. Another brother, Joseph, continued to farm in Kingham, at least until 1835.

Michael did return on a visit to England and married Martha Moore. They seem to have lived at Begbroke House for a while but they returned to VDL, where they had two daughters, Martha and Annie. In February 1854 he took his family to England for a visit, sailing on the *Derwent Water*. They lived in the Glenorchy suburb of Hobart until his death on 29 November 1888. His nephew, also Michael, son of Joseph, also emigrated aged 21 and lived with his uncle and then his aunt Jane. He married in 1860.[cxiii]

It is worth noting that Michael Steel emigrated at very much the same time as clan leader, Cameron of Lochiel, who acquired significant lands i.e. some 100,000 acres, in the Ross area of VDL, and over 100 staff (?convicts). This seems to show how keen VDL was to encourage emigrants at the time.

b. Alfred Joy – from Oxford to Melbourne, 1853-54

The diary of Alfred Joy survives in the Oxfordshire History Centre but there is very limited information about him or his wife available or how the diary ended up in the Centre. In the 1851 census Alfred Joy was a tailor-partner in Oxford, with two servants. On 23 December 1852, he married Henrietta Julia Carlina Solari (born c.1829) in Lambeth. His diary covers their voyage from London and during their early settlement in Melbourne, from 25 April 1853 to 29 June 1854 (only page 1 is missing).

They sailed from Gravesend in the barque *Thamas Harrison*, with 17 unassisted passengers on board, including 13 'tween-deck passengers', and the Surgeon, Frederick George Howard (32). The voyage lasted 155 days and they docked in Melbourne on 22 September 1853. Here are some excerpts from the diary:

1853

8 May, The ship sprung the Mainmast and they were forced to spend a fortnight in Lisbon. During this time, he went to a Bull Fight and went on board the Firebrand War Steamer and the Agamemnon, Man of War with 92 guns.

27 July, He saw a large quantity of Albatrosses and a school of whales, and next day caught 3 Cape Pigeons (CPs) and an Albatross. The Doctor offered to skin it but instead he decided to send it and 2 CPs to Tom [?his brother]!

5 August, After passing the Cape of Good Hope, about 200 miles to the south, they experienced very heavy gales, which swamped the cabin and berths and carried away about 5 yards of the bulwarks, later another 2 yards and the top of the Binnicle [box on deck holding the compass]. Water in the cabin much deeper than is pleasant.

19 August, Out of most stores, and we have killed and eaten all the sheep, pigs and poultry.

20 August, Terrible day, ship 'hoved to' and run before the wind. Long boat, Water cask & spare spars broke from their lashings and I gave ourselves up for lost. The bulwarks are nearly all gone and a son of one of the deck passengers was nearly washed over board. 'I hope I shall never witness another such day'.

11 September, Nearly calm.

20 September, Pilot on board and dropped anchor at Port Phillip Heads. about 1pm.

22 September, New pilot and sailed for Hobsons Bay (about 30 miles), where we dropped anchor at 4pm, after a tedious voyage of 155 days. Clearing Officer came on board and claimed acquaintance with me, he proved to be Mr Charles Broad, a nephew at Bidgoods [probably the Oxford tailors where Joy worked], he invited me to his home, at Williamstown on bank of Hobsons Bay, about 8 miles from Melbourne. I slept at his house the first night. [This was the first of many acquaintances he met].

23 September, to Melbourne by steamer. Delivered some of my letters of introduction and heard from Mr Hugh Walker that he had letters for me from home. Met Tom Brazier.

25 September, Went to Church with Mrs Broad, who afterwards accompanied her husband on board, to dine with us. She is a funny little woman, 16 years old and has been married 3 years.

4 October, Henrietta confined of a Boy at 20 minutes before one in the morning.

16 October, The *Great Britain* arrived.

18 October, Saw land in N.Melbourne, about 1 mile from Post Office, with tolerable road. Settled for the purchase & bought a pick & shovel to commence tomorrow.

19 October, Shouldered my pick and shovel and turned the first sod on my estate.

21 October, Went with the Doctor to North Melbourne to commence erecting our 'Iron House'.

25 October, Finished the house with the exception of fastening on the roof.

1854

3 January, A hot wind and the thermometer at 110 in the shade. Today has been the hottest day since Black Thursday so that so many people died. The country is all in flames with the bush fires for miles around.

6 January, Met Stephen Burstall of University College, Oxford, and invited him to dine with me on Sunday.

8 January, Mr Burstall came. He has been at the Diggings ever since he arrived here, until the last 10 days. He has not been very successful, but he had a Gold Commissionership offered to him.

18 January, Started fishing at half past 12. The moon was well up, so that I could see sufficiently well to keep out of the gullies. The fish bit well and I caught 36 bream. [He fished very regularly and always caught a good number e.g. 46 mullet and 20 trout (1 Feb) and 22 bream before breakfast on 3 Feb].

23 January, Henrietta went to Mr Walkers at Collingwood and I called for her in the evening. [This was a regular visit for one or both of them]

6 February, Had an offer from Mr Bliss to go to his office at 2 pounds per week till something better turns up.

10 March, I was amused, when in the Bank this morning, by seeing a Black Man, dressed in the most stylish manner and one of the Clerks addressing him with "Well Mr Lane, what can I do for you", he quietly answered, "Oh I only want a couple thousand this morning". I find he is the owner of a Public House and reputed to be immensely rich. I am very comfortable with Mr Bliss, he gives me 4 pounds per week, and as the business increases he will make it better for me.

27 April, Dined with Mrs Thomas and met several young from Kingston-on-

Thames, all of whom knew her at Walkam and Hellamche, out here now. [A gap in the diary from here until 23 June]

23 June, The *"Queen of the South"* came in, with the long expected Governor on board.

24 June, A general holiday to enable everyone to go and welcome the Governor. These excerpts show how many introductions he seems to have had and how organized he was in advance. His social life picks up immediately and he soon has a job to tide him over until something better turns up. He is also very quick to buy land and build an 'Iron House' in October and November. Later records show him living in Hawthorne, Melbourne in November 1858 and he dies in 1878, aged 55, in Victoria (no place given). Henrietta died in 1881, age 51, at Collingwood, Melbourne (a northern suburb), where they had chosen to live in 1854. No further information about the Joys has to come to light.[cxiv]

c. The Butler Family – from Fringford to Queensland, 1869-74

Four brothers in the Butler family, all born in Fringford, emigrated to Queensland from 1869-74. Henry, who had moved from Mackay to Townsville, also purchased a small sailing boat and would sail to Magnetic Island on weekends, where he built a 'log and slab hut with a thatched roof and was the first white settler among the local aborigines.' He was joined there by his brothers Charles and Thomas after they arrived in 1874. In 1877, Henry brought his family to the Island, where they lived for 21 years. He died in 1924 but his daughter, Ellen, continued to live on the Island until her death in 1958.

Charles and Thomas 'erected a lime kiln, where they burnt coral and later freighted it in its powered [powdered] form in their sailing boat to Townsville. Also from this they built their own coral house which was still in existence in 1938.' Thomas left the Island and moved further north to Mackay to work as a line repair man and in 1896 he was transferred to the post office in Cardwell. In 1900, he purchased some 168 acres, of land, house, and fruit trees in Murray Upper (the upper reaches of the Murray River). The property was then called 'Blechynden' which Thomas changed to 'Fringford.' Joseph also moved to Murray Upper in 1900, where he and his wife, Emma, managed the property until Thomas and his family moved there from Cardwell about 1902. Joseph then bought a property across the creek from 'Fringford', where he built a house called 'Yabbon' and farmed the land and bred cattle and horses until his death in 1909.

At the 'Fringford' farm, Thomas grew maize and bananas, raised fowls and pigs, and bred cattle and horses. All the produce was taken by horse-wagon to Cardwell for shipment to southern Australia, and they collected their groceries on the return trip. The whole trip took two or three days and at night they camped out on the side of the road. In 1926, Thomas took up post office work again on

Crossing the Murray River, Northern Queensland, the Butler family: Rowdy (Hugh),
Ormie, Florence and Aunty (May?), c.1910. (Rhonda Smith).

Picnic Aussie Style, Outback, Northern Queensland, the Butler family c.1910.
(Rhonda Smith).

Fringford Working Party, Northern Queensland, the Butler family,
L to R, R.B. Blackman, Hugh R. Butler, T. Ormie, c.1910
(Rhonda Smith).

the Murray River, and his son, Ormand, began the first motorized Royal Mail
Service with a Model T Ford truck. Thomas lived on at 'Fringford' until his death
in 1948. Electricity was not connected to the Murray District and 'Fringford' until
1974. None of Thomas's children married and like him they were all buried on
the property, except for Hugh Ramsey, who was killed in action in France on 28
November 1916 while rescuing a friend.

The 'Fringford' log and slab hut was occupied until the last member of the
family, Mr Shirley Butler, died in 1976. He was befriended by a fellow called John
Ryan, who inherited 'Fringford' and he stripped it bare. He then sold it to the
man who was running a historical village centre called Romana Land in Cardwell.
The project was a failure and subsequently 'Fringford' and the centre all burnt to
the ground. So there was a sad end to 'Fringford' but the Butler family certainly
played their part in the history of the early pioneers. The emigration experience
had its challenges for the brothers but they were welcomed as immigrants,
encouraged to buy land in areas which had never been developed and they were
their own masters. It was all a far cry from working in England in the 1870s, on
the railway or on the land, for very modest wages of some 11s (55p) or 12 s (60p)
a week. It is very unlikely that they had any regrets at their decision to
emigrate.[cxv]

Thomas, Henry and Charles Butler, Magnetic Island, Northern Queensland,
early 1920s (Rhonda Smith).

Fringford Farm, Murray Upper, Northern Queensland, 1920s (Rhonda Smith).

d. Emigrants from West Oxfordshire, to New Zealand, 1873-74

A group from West Oxfordshire sailed on the *Inverene* to Hawkes Bay in November 1873. They in the main took up and cleared forest country, and included the following members:

John Mycock, 44, of Charlbury, his wife, Sarah, and six children. By 1882, he was farming 68 acres of his own worth £250 at Ormandville.

Edward Harding of Taynton, his wife, Sarah, and 5 children. By 1882, he owned 144 acres of freehold at Woodville worth £1,136, on which he was running 295 sheep by 1883.

John Ireland of Milton-under-Wychwood, wife, Phillis, and 11 children and 2 grandchildren owned 108 acres at Makaretu in 1882.

John Penfold, Secretary of the Taynton branch of NALU, sailed on the *Hudson* in November 1874, and also settled in Woodville.

The Woodville Settlement, founded in 1875, had a strong Oxfordshire contingent, including the Hardings and others from the *Inverene*, among them their daughter and son in law, Henry and Frances Cox, and Edward and Eliza Groves, and their six children, all from Milton-under-Wychwood.

In 1874, the following also arrived from the Wychwoods:

a. Peter and Millicent Honeybourne, of Ascott-under-Wychwood, brought their 8 year old son, Thomas. Thirty years later he was running the carrying business which his father had established at Waikiri in Canterbury - with 3 waggons, 2 spring drays, a gig, and a tip cart.

b. Henry Hutt, 6 year old son of James and Esther Hutt of Charlbury, was appointed manager of Paeroa Creamery in Auckland in 1899.

c. Charles Barnes, 14, came out with his parents, Thomas and Ann. By 1899, he was combining farming with running an agricultural contracting business for which he had a 'complete agricultural plant'.

All the above men were labourers and in a few years were freeholders. This seems to show how successful emigration could be for those brave enough to undertake the long journey to New Zealand in the 1870s.

e. Annie Saunders from Cubbington, near Leamington, to Canada, 1906.

As noted above, Annie Saunders (née Shaylor) was born in 1869 at Cubbington, where she graduated as a nurse at the Warneford Hospital in 1885. In 1906 she emigrated to Cobalt in Northern Ontario, Canada. Cobalt was a mining town which was only reachable by rail or boat, and the water route was impassable for six months in winter. Her brother was already there and he had encouraged her to come to recover from ill health. Cobalt was big international news since one of the largest discoveries of silver in 1903, which lasted into the 1920s. There were some 100 mines in and around Cobalt.

On 18 May 1906, there was an explosion of a dynamite magazine and Annie lost everything. Her house was rebuilt and her front room was used a hospital, There were three doctors but she was the only nurse. In 1906, the mine owners built a new hospital with Annie as the administrator. In 1909, there was the largest typhoid outbreak ever in Ontario, and 100 nurses came north from Toronto. In 1915, Annie went back to England and nursed in World War One from 1916 to 1919. She then went to Vancouver, where she joined her husband and one of her sons before going on to California to join her other son. She then returned to Lindsey, Ontario. In 1931, she finally returned to Cubbington, where she continued to nurse until her death in 1932 aged 64. This maybe only one story of an emigrant among so many but it does reveal the strength and determination of a lady who suffered some ill health in her early life. Her many moves also shed some light on the possible mobility at the time.

Chapter 9

Conclusion

Until the end of the Napoleonic Wars in 1815, the story was largely about transportation of convicts and penal colonies and not emigration. It was Captain Cook's voyages from 1768 to 1775 which opened up the possibility of colonies in Australasia. He completed a chart of New Zealand and claimed the whole of the east coast of Australia for King George III. After the social unrest and widespread Poor Law problems in the 1820s, the government changed their attitude to emigration, passed the Poor Law Amendment Act of 1834, and urged the Poor Law unions to encourage it. Farm labourers, most of whom had never even left their own parishes, were generally very conservative and slow to realize the possibilities of a better life which emigration could offer them. The Act of 1834 provided real encouragement to the Poor Law unions and to the farm labourers, and we have seen the extent of emigration in the Four Shires after it. It was the Durham Report of 1839 which, after its adoption in 1846, made the most dramatic change to the government's relationship with the white colonies. It was this and the Repeal of the Corn Laws, also in 1846, which led to the Great Exodus and the growth of the Victorian Empire.

The early voyages to Australia, all on sailing ships, were long and very uncomfortable, and brought serious risk of disease, notably cholera and typhoid. There is plenty of evidence to show how tough these early voyages could be. There were many deaths, particularly of young children, and improvements in the passages were slow and the health risks continued into the 1870s. There were also risks to the ships and a number of disasters, including those of the *Cataraqui* and the *Cospatrick*, where there was serious loss of local lives. The Great Exodus followed after 1850, by which time many sailing ships also had auxiliary steam engines powered by a single screw, which made 75-80 days a realistic target for the Australia run. By the 1870s, steamships were regularly carrying emigrants to Australia, although sailing ships continued to the end of the 19th century. Between 1871 and 1911, some six million emigrated, most of them men from rural areas, so that by 1900 there were over one million more women than men in Britain. Many of them saw it as a search for 'The Promised Land', and free land was often on offer from Canada, New Zealand and Australia, as noted in the *Bicester Advertiser* at the time. In August 1872, the Queensland Government took the bold step of offering entirely free passages to approved agricultural labourers and their wives and children, with the virtual certainty of jobs being available for them on arrival. By doing so, Queensland was able to secure large numbers of labourers, who could never have afforded to pay even part of their fares themselves.

It is to be hoped that the above has given some idea of the extent and nature of emigration from Oxfordshire and its neighbours in the period from 1815 to 1914. In the early years, particularly before the invention of the steam engine. the prospect of the long, uncomfortable, and dangerous passages in sailing ships must have been very daunting for potential emigrants. Most of them were agricultural labourers, who had barely even left their own parishes. It was a long walk to Liverpool for a start, and the hustle and bustle of the big city must have been terrifying. There were all sorts of risks from rogue sellers of lodgings and passages, and all the supposed requirements for the journey. Improved protection was provided later by emigration agents and ship owners but it must have been very confusing for these naïve farm labourers. That said, life for most of them in their new countries seems to have been a success and better than their prospects staying in England. The Butlers and their descendents, for example, prospered, in comparison to what they might have expected in England. They, and so many others, also made a major contribution to the growth of the colonies. Tribute must be paid to Lord Durham for his Report and to the Russell Government for adopting it as imperial policy. It was this that led to a long-term peaceful relationship with the colonies and the growth of the Victorian Empire. As James Morris suggested, there are mixed views on the Victorian Empire but there were undoubted benefits, not just for the United Kingdom, in the development of shipping, railways, emigration and the colonies.

Epilogue

On a personal note, I am aware of a number of my own family who emigrated in the 19th century. Charles Greenwood and his brother, John, emigrated to the United States in May 1850 and settled in Rush Court Farm, Aztalan in Jefferson County, Wisconsin. In 1860, Arthur Greenwood, another brother, also emigrated to Wisconsin. In 1883, Charles Frederick Greenwood, and his brother Arthur Wellington, two sons of Charles (who had died in 1881), opened Greenwood Brothers, Bankers in Lake Mills. In 1893, this became Greenwood's State Bank, which is still flourishing today with a number of branches. In 1852, William Augustus Greenwood, another brother of Charles, emigrated to Australia but returned to England c.1875. In the late 1920s, three Greenwood sisters emigrated to Vancouver Island in British Columbia to teach at Queen Margaret's School in Duncan. Bella returned to England in 1936 and in 1937 she played cricket for England Ladies against Australia, the first such game. She then served in the Second World War, before returning to her teaching job in Canada. In 1980, the sisters were joined by their younger brother, Alexander who also moved to Vancouver Island. In 1954, Dr Kemble Greenwood emigrated to Victoria, British Columbia, and most of his descendents still live there. In 1960 my sister, Gillian Seager, went to Montreal and in 1962 she and Douglas moved to Vancouver, where she still lives.

In the summer of 1940, when England was suffering the worst of the Blitz, my mother with my sister and myself came very close to moving to the United States. A surviving telegram from a Greenwood cousin dated 30 July 1940 reads as follows:' Immediately get visitors passport for New York airplane Communicate my nephew Ira Bird New York Times meet you Can we help others. Arthur Greenwood'. Accomodation was available with Arthur in California or in his house in Wisconsin. My father's reply indicates that immediate departure was impossible and his notes reveal that there were no flights available for at least two months. His draft reply shows that he and my mother had decided that the Germans were unlikely to be strong enough to mount an invasion, and the family was safe in the Worcestershire countryside. So we came that close to living in the Promised Land for some five years.

In the summer of 1957, I went to Canada with a university group. We all went our several ways, and I hitch- hiked some 3,000 miles each way across the continent, as far as Vancouver Island, where I stayed with Kemble Greenwood and his family for a couple of months. On my return journey through the United

States, I called in at Lake Mills and stayed briefly with Charles Frederick, the 5th President of the Greenwood State Bank. He retired in 1971 bringing to a close the family connection of over 87 years of banking in Lake Mills.

On this trip, I experienced something like 'The Promised Land' both in Canada and the United States. Apart from the revelation of the sheer size and grandeur of the two countries, I experienced the kindness of so many who gave me lifts, made diversions to show me special places, and even the ride with an Arkansas lorry driver, where we were barely able to understand each other. As a visitor, I was always welcomed, and sometimes invited to drive their cars. In Victoria, I worked for a roofing gang, where they suffered my incompetence and helped me to improve. Later, in the 1960s and 1970s, I spent a year in the United States and twelve years in Vancouver and Ottawa, before returning to the UK. So I did get to enjoy The Promised Land.

Appendix 1

A List of the Oxfordshire Emigrants Lost in the Wreck of the Cataraqui, 4 August 1845

Chesterton (2)
William Andrews (240
Maria Andrews (26)

Fringford (7)
Joseph Cotterill (22)
Martha Cotterill (20)
George Cotterill (2)
Elisa Cotterill (infant)
Thomas White (25)
Anne White (23)
Hanna Figge (3)

Fritwell (4)
William Rutter (25)
Fanny Rutter (25)
Matilda Rutter (2)
Mary Rutter (1)

Great Haseley (7)
Charles Knott (39)
Rebecca Knott (40)
Joseph Knottt (14)
Charles Knott (10)
Anne Knott (8)
Rebecca Knott (6)
James Knott (2)

Kiddington (9)
William Simmonds (33)
Deborah Simmonds (32)
Mary Anne Simmonds (12)
Paul Savings (11)
Patience Savings (11)
H. William Savings (10)
Emma Savings (7)
John Savings (3)
John Simmonds (infant)

Rousham (1)
Emily Walton (18)

Stoke Lyne (5)
Mary Anne Loveridge (27)
John Loveridge (21)
George Watts (27)
Elizabeth Watts (25)
Richard Watts (infant)

Stonefield (15)
William Barrett (38)
Mary Barrett (39)
George Barrett (10)
Dinah Barrett (9)
Henry Barrett (7)
Francis Barrett (6)
Hanna Rawlins (39)
James Oliver (20)
James Rawlins (45)
Caroline Rawlins (18)
Sarah Rawlins (16)
Emily Rawlins (13)
Henry Rawlins (9)
William Rawlins (6)
Francis Rawlins (2)

Tackley (42)
James Cook (27)
Anne Cook (23)
Mary Cook (5)
June Cook (2)
John Cook (infant)
William Cook (39)
Anne Cook (36)
Mary Anne Cook (15)
Sarah Cook (11)
Francis Cook (6)

Tackley (cont)
Richard Cook (5)
John Cook (3)
William Cook (infant)
Stephen Floyd (26)
Hanna Floyd (25)
Mary Anne Floyd ((2)
Willima Floyd (infant)
Robert Hoare (26)
Emma Hoare (23)
Thomas Hoare (2)
Millicent Hoare (infant)
Antony Merry (37)
Edith Merry (36)
Martha Merry (16)
Joseph Merry (14)
John Merry (13)
William Merry (10)
James Merry (9)
Emma Merry (7)
Rhoda Merry (5)
Matthew Merry (3)
Susan Merry (infant)
John Ryman (29)
Hannah Ryman (26)
James Harwood (8)
Joseph Ryman (5)
Mary Jane Ryman (infant)
John Savings (33)
Sarah Savings (35)
Elisabeth Payne (5)
Frederick Payne (4)
Philip Savings (infant)

Wootton (4)
William Bishop (38)
Hanna Bishop
Sarah Bishop (16)
Elizabeth Bishop (13)

Total: 96 from Oxfordshire of 399 lost in the shipwreck.

Appendix 2

The Durham Report

By a stroke of good fortune, my neighbour's great-grandfather, John Richard Coke-Smyth, a distinguished artist, was drawing master to Lord Durham when he went to Canada in 1839 as Governor General of British North America. This led me to borrowing *Letters and Diaries of Lady Durham* and *The Diary of Jane Ellice*, wife of Edward Ellice, who was Lord Durham's Private Secretary. Both these diaries were written in 1839-40 but not published until the 1970s in Canada. They provide a fascinating glimpse into the life of Lord Durham as he tried to bring peace to Canada after the rebellion of 1837. It is clear that Durham's tact and courtesy to visiting Americans and Canadians of all factions made a great impression on all those who came into contact with him. As noted above, however, his most serious problems lay at home with his enemies in the Tory Party, notably the Lord Brougham. In Canada, his most urgent and delicate problem was how to deal with the political prisoners arrested during the 1837 rebellion. Nearly 500 had been seized and about two thirds of these had been released. The difficulty with the remaining third was that if they were brought to trial in Lower Canada, French Canadian juries there would acquit them.

Lord Durham solved the problem with a decision that was accepted with general approval in Canada. In his ordinance, the eight principal leaders were banished to Bermuda, on pain of death if they returned. The remaining 153 were released. This was better than the French Canadians had hoped for, but at the same time the ring leaders were removed from the scene. In the House of Lords, however, Lord Brougham vigorously protested the illegality of this action. He argued that the eight men could not be banished without trial, nor could Durham threaten them with death if they should return to their own land. In spite of general agreement that his decision was a sensible one, the government was not prepared to pass supplementary legislation to justify it. Thus the illegality of Durham's ordinance could not be denied and he had no choice but to resign.

The following items from Lady Durham's *Letters and Diary of 1838* shed some interesting light on Lord Durham's Mission:

Tuesday 17 July, 'Military Review at Niagara Falls was attended by a great number of Americans who came over from Buffalo etc. The Officer highest in rank on the Frontier, Major [Young] was received by Him {Durham} & attended to all the morning with great civility, & was requested to stay for dinner & a dance afterwards with as many of his countrymen as he might like to invite... About 30 (I think) accepted the invitation.. We dined about 4 o'clock, sitting down about 200. ...It was the first occasion on which any attempt towards cordiality had been made on the part of a British Commander, & the result completely answered his [Durham's] expectations. From that moment a marked change took place in the feeling of the People of the United States, & for the first time good will & a friendly spirit seemed to prevail among them towards the English of the Colonies.'

13 Sept, 'we have seen the account of what passed in Parl. on Canada affairs after the news of the ordinances. I have not words to express what I think of the wickedness of Ld. Brougham's conduct – in gratifying his malicious spite he is quite indifferent as to the mischief he may do here. In this I trust he has overacted his part, but that makes no alteration in one's opinion of him.'

19 September, 'He had received a bag of letters & despatches from England containing the account of the *reception of* the ordinances, with private letters from Lord Melbourne & others rejoicing over the manner in which the difficult affair of the Prisoners had been settled, & bidding him "go & prosper", with other expressions of unqualified approbation.' What could have been more gratifying than these communications! But a New York paper, with later intelligence from home, reversed all these visions of success, and contained the account of the proceedings of Parl! The disallowance of the ordinances! &, as it proved, the doom of his fate. The most violent language was openly held on the streets, separation from England talked of, & it was said that it would be better to be connected with the United States than with a country which was so reckless of the interests of its Colonies. ..One general feeling of disapprobation & regret at what had occurred.. & the first impression of all, on hearing the news, was that he would not, could not stay; that he must resign & go home instantly. Subsequently these opinions may have been in some measure altered; the country generally was most anxious that he should remain but all his advisers ..were decided that his stay was impossible.'

Wednesday, 26 September, 'He received the official account of what had passed in parlt, but no private letters from the Ministers explaining or attempting to excuse their conduct. Subsequently he had a letter from Lord John Russell... but this was the only private communication He received from any one connected with the Govt.'

9 October, 'He published, as directed from home, the disallowance of the ordinances, & the Act of Indemnity, &, at the same time, His own famous Proclamation explaining & justifying His conduct, & giving his reason for leaving the Colony. This took place at an immense meeting in the Chamber of the H. of Assembly, at which he was presented an address from the Inhabitants of Quebec signed by 4,287 names. There had never been so large a meeting in Canada. ..It is to be supposed that He was much affected by the testimonies of respect & confidence which he received on all sides from the People of Canada. He labored incessantly till He had completed the *Report,* which amply redeemed the Pledge to the People of Canada.'

18 *October,* 'It had been intended that the *Inconstant* should go round to meet us at New York, & we should have gone to Washington etc. But he thinks it right to proceed home with as little delay as possible, in order to lay before the Government the critical state of the Provinces. (Had he been able to carry into effect the visit to the United States, He would have been received with the greatest honours which had ever been paid to any individual except La Fayette. He would have been lodged in the *White House* & considered as the nation's guest). The *Inconstant* sailed for England on 1 November but due to rough weather did not land at Devonport until 30 November.'

1 *December,* He was not able to take part in the Session of '40, but he saw the triumph of His views for Canada {including the union of Upper and Lower Canada}, & could foresee the success of His principles. Justice is as yet but imperfectly done to him, at least in England, but the time may come when he will be better appreciated.' How very true!

The Diary of Jane Ellice

Edward Ellice, the Younger (1810-1880), became Private Secretary to Lord Durham. He was the son of Edward 'Bear' Ellice (1781-1863), a highly influential member of the Whig party, closely associated drawing up the Reform Bill of 1832. Bear's father, Alexander, had invested extensively in land in the northern United States and in Canada, In 1810, it was estimated that he owned approximately 133,970 acres in New England, some 280,000 acres (with about 16,000 adjacent acres) in the seignory of Beauharnois, on the south bank of the St Lawrence west of Montreal, and considerable acreage in Prince Edward Island. He also had extensive business and shipping interests in connection with the West Indies. So the family's advice on Canadian matters was highly influential, but could not be said to be entirely impartial. On the night of 3 November, armed French Canadian rebels attacked the seignory taking Edward and the other male occupants into the bush as prisoners, while his wife, Jane , and her sister Tina, together with other British settlers, were kept captive in the house. They were rescued on 10 November and Edward returned safely on the next day. Quite an experience for them all!

Appendix 3

Cornish Emigration

Although Cornish emigration does not form a part of this study, Cornwall did experience its own 'Great Exodus' between 1815 and 1914, and it provides an interesting comparison with the four shires. Although many Cornish emigrants in the 19th century were farmers or agricultural labourers, the majority were out-of-work miners, who had 'their highly developed sense of superiority'. It was on the new mining frontiers of America, Australia and South Africa that pride in Cornish industrial prowess gave birth to the 'myth' of Cousin Jack, the belief that the Cornish were innately and uniquely equipped as skilled hard-rock miners. In America, it was the lead mining regions of Wisconsin and Illinois, together with the burgeoning copper country of the Lakes and (later) the iron oesota, which provided important sources of employment at a time when economic downturn in Cornwall had combined with potato blight to perpetuate the Great Exodus. Free or assisted passages drew them to Cape Colony, New South Wales, New Zealand and other British colonies, and also to Peru, Mexico and Chile. In 1849, the Gold Rush in California led to many Cornishmen moving there, as they were preferred to the Mexican miners.

A great many of these Cornish emigrants went to Canada and the United States between 1831 and 1860. The ports of Liverpool and London necessitated a long journey for them, certainly before the railways. Ports on the north and south coasts of Cornwall and Devon were therefore important points of departure; these included Padstow, Fowey, Truro, Falmouth, Penzance and St Ives, together with Plymouth and Bideford in Devon. From Padstow alone, some 6,200 emigrants sailed to Canada in those years. In 1841, Padstow was the third most important departure point for Canada, surpassed only by Liverpool and London. The potato crop was said to be 'the principal staff of Cornish life' but the crop failed in 1845 and 1846, leading to food riots, and emigration proved to be the impetus. This was helped by the newly-discovered copper deposits in Michigan and of copper in South Australia at Kapunda in 1843-44, Burra Burra in 1845, and the discoveries in 1861 at Moonta, which became known as 'Australia's Little Cornwall'. In the period 1862 to 1870 over thirteen thousand immigrants were recorded in South Australia's shipping passenger lists. No fewer than a quarter of these was from Cornwall, and in 1865 an extraordinary 43% of arrivals were Cornish.

Cornish studies have shown the amazing mobility of many of these miners, who moved easily, for example, from America to Australia and back again seeking the best jobs. However, they tended to keep close ties with Cornwall and, importantly, 'homepay', the remittances sent home, supported large sections of the community. This was particularly true after the 'Crashed Copper' in 1866 and the 'Tumbling Tin' in the mid-1870s. Many of these emigrants, particularly to South Australia, were Wesleyans, Primitive Methodists and Bible Christians, the last group a Methodist denomination founded in North Cornwall in 1815, who all sought to recreate their religious communities overseas. By the 1850s, 'at least half of the population [of Australia] were Irish Catholics, Scottish Presbyterians or Cornish Methodists'.

This demonstrates how much Cornwall contributed to the story of emigration from 1815 to 1914. The peaks in Cornish emigration were very much at the same time as in the Oxfordshire area, although their problems were mostly related to agriculture, while the Cornish ones were related to mining.[cxvi]

Bibliography

Primary Sources

John H.Hillary, *Westland, the Journal of John Hillary, Emigrant to New Zealand* (James Publishing, 1995).

Alfred Joy, *The Diary of Alfred Joy, 1853-54* (unpublished, Oxfordshire History Centre).

Joseph Sams, *The Diary of Joseph Sams,* (HMSO, 1982).

Published Sources

M.K.Ashby, *Joseph Ashby of Tysoe 1859-1019, A Study of English Village Life* (Cambridge University Press, 1961).

Stephen Bates, *Two Nations, Britain in 1846* (Head of Zeus, 2015).

J.C.Blomfield, *Deanery of Bicester, Part 11, History of Bicester* (1884).

Kevin Brown, *Passage to the World, The Emigrant Experience 1807-1940* (Seaforth, 2013).

Vanessa Collingridge, *Captain Cook, Obsession and Betrayal in the New World* (Ebury Press, 2003).

David John Douglass, *A History of the Liverpool Waterfront, 1850-1890, The Struggle for Organisation* (Fonthill, 2013).

Jeremy Gibson, *Sponsored Emigration of Paupers from Banbury Union, 1834-1860* (Oxford Family Society, 1982, v.2: no.7 (1982 Spring), pp.211-215).

Martin Greenwood, *The Real Candleford Green, The Story of a Lark Rise Village* (Robert Boyd Publications, 2016).

David Hey, *Family & Local History in England* (Longman, 1987).

Patricia Godsell (ed), *Letters & Diaries of Lady Durham* (Oberon Press, Canada, 1979).

Patricia Godsell (ed), *The Diary of Jane Ellice* (Oberon Press, Canada, 1975).

Pamela Horn, *Agricultural Trade Unionism and Emigration, 1872-1881* (The Historical Journal, xv, 1 (1972), pp.87-102).

Roger Kershaw and Mark Pearsall, *Family History, On the Move, Where your ancestors went and why* (The National Archives, 2006).

Matthew Kneale, *English Passengers,* (Penguin, 2001).

Catherine Lorigan, *Delabole, The History of the Slate Quarry and the Making of the Village Community* (Pengelly Press, 2007).

Barry McKay, *Tackley to Tasmania, Pauper Emigration from an Oxfordshire Village to Australia,* and the *Wreck of the Cataraqui, 1845* (1992).

John Milburn & Keith Jarrott, *The Aylesbury Agitator, Edward Richardson: Labourers' Friend and Queensland Agent, 1849-1878* (Milburn & Jarrott, 1988).

G.E.Mingay, *Rural Life in Victorian England* (Alan Sutton, 1990).

James Morris, *Heaven's Command, An Imperial Progress* (Penguin, 1979).

James Morris, *Pax Britannica, The Climax of an Empire* (Penguin, 1979).

James Morris, *Farewell the Trumpets, An Imperial Retreat* (Penguin, 1979).

Philip Payton, *The Cornish Overseas, The epic story of the 'Great Emigration'* (University Press of Exeter, 2005).

Philip Payton, *Making Moonta, The Invention of Australia's Little Cornwall* (University Press of Exeter, 2007).

Kate Tiller and Giles Darkes (ed), *An Historical Atlas of Oxfordshire* (Oxfordshire Record Society, Volume 67, 2010).

The Victoria History of the Counties of England, A History of Oxfordshire, Volumes 1-XV.

Notes

Chapter 1 Captain Cook, Transportation and Penal Colonies

[i] Article by Lucy Davies in the *Daily Telegraph* on 25 April 2018, quoting Vanessa Collingridge, prior to the British Library's Exhibition commemorating 250 years since Cook first set sail.

[ii] Roger Kershaw and Mark Pearsall, *Family History, On the Move, Where your ancestors went and why*, 144-5 (The National Archives, 2006).

[iii] Transportation figures from Kershaw, ibid., 173.

[iv] Philip Payton, *The Cornish Overseas, The epic story of the 'Great Emigration'*, 75.

[v] *Sentences of Transportation from Oxfordshire Courts, 1787-1867*, Compiled by Carol Richmond (2007).

[vi] Eric and Margaret Smith, Victoria, Australia.

Chapter 2 Major Emigrant Settlements

[vii] David Hey, *Family & Local History in England*, 80 (Longman, 1987).

[viii] James Morris, *Heaven's Command, An Imperial Progress*, 141-7.

[ix] *The Diary of Joseph Sams*, 58.

[x] Scyld Berry in the *Daily Telegraph*, 9 March 2018.

[xi] James Morris, op. cit., 143.

[xii] Scyld Berry, op.cit.

[xiii] *Brogdens' Navvies, Brogden Family History*, based on Rollo Arnold's *The Farthest Promised Land*.

[xiv] Pauline Ashbridge, *Children of Dissent*, 1-5 (2008).

[xv] Juliet Gardiner & Neil Wenborn, *The History Today Companion to British History*, 595 (1995).

Chapter 3 Social Unrest and Poor Law Problems

[xvi] *The History Today Companion to British History*, 696.

[xvii] David Newsome, *The Victorian World Picture*, 42 (1997).

[xviii] David Newsome, op.cit., 235.

[xix] *British History*, op.cit., 710.

[xx] Blomfield, *Deanery of Bicester*, Part II, 48-9 (1884).

[xxi] 1837, Warwickshire : Board of Guardians – Shipston Union (WRO 00607).

[xxii] Audrey M. Taylor, *Gilletts, Bankers at Banbury and Oxford*, 109-10.

[xxiii] Stephen Bates, *Two Nations, Britain in 1846*, 306.

Chapter 4 Emigration from Oxfordshire and neighbouring Buckinghamshire, Northamptonshire and Warwickshire

xxiv Most of this information comes from *An Historical Atlas of Oxfordshire*, by Kate Tiller and Giles Darkes (ed) (Oxfordshire Record Society Vol 67, 2010).

xxv Jeremy Gibson, *Sponsored Emigration of Paupers from Banbury Union, 1834-60*, and the *Victoria County History of Oxfordshire*.

xxvi Audrey M.Taylor, *Gilletts, Bankers at Banbury and Oxford*, 109-10 (OUP 1964).

xxvii Audrey M.Taylor, ibid., 110.

xxviii Dr J.Blencowe, *Assisted Emigration of Paupers from Bicester in 1830*, 86-93 (Oxfordshire Family History, Vol 8 No.2, Summer 1994).

xxix Blomfield, op.cit., 50,

xxx Brian Jackson, *Early Emigrants from Chilterns Area to Victoria* (Oxfordshire Family History, Vol 8 No.2, Summer 1994).

xxxi Barry McKay, *Tackley to Tasmania, Pauper Emigration from an Oxfordshire Village to Australia, and The Wreck of the Cataraqui*, 1845 (1992).

xxxii Eric and Margaret Smith, Victoria, Australia.

xxxiii Betty Chandler, *From Oxfordshire by Assisted Passengers Scheme to Milthorpe, NSW Australia* (Oxfordshire Family History, Vol 9, No.1 Spring 1995).

xxxiv Memo of Great Linford parish, 15 February 1844 (NRO, D-U/8/3/8).

xxxv Letter from Thomas Drew to Fdk Druce, 1 December, 1848 (NRO, PR247/19/11).

xxxvi Notice of Meeting in Woughton Parish, 9 December 1848 (NRO, PR247/19/12).

xxxvii Circular to the Overseers of the parish of Warkworth, 9 June 1836 (NRO, 341P/035).

xxxviii Syd Tyrrell, *A Countryman's Tale*, 77-9 (1973).

xxxix Dr J.Blencowe, op.cit,, 84-6.

xl Broughton expenses of emigration, 6 December 1850 (NRO, G(K)299).

xli Letter from Revd Brown re Free Passage to South Australia, 18 August 1838 (NRO, NPL1708).

xlii Expenses of Faulkners and party from Pytchley, 12 March 1844 (NRO, NPL1657).

xliii Letter to Revd A.W.Brown, 28 January 1846 (NRO, NPL/1651).

xliv Final list of expenses for emigration, 30 July 1850 (NRO, NPL/1649).

xlv Kettering Poor Law Board Authorisation, 1 May 1849 (NRO, G(K)/298).

xlvi Printed 'Notice to Young Women', 19 Jan 1833 (WCRO, DRO583/98/1-3).

xlvii Report to the Colonial Secretary of State on Emigration to the Australian Colonies, 1834-5, (WCRO, DR362/117/105).

xlviii Wellesbourne Parish papers, 1830s-1840s (WCRO, CR1596/box120-4/44/4).

xlix Jeremy Gibson, op.cit.

l M.K.Ashby, *Joseph Ashby of Tysoe, 1859-1919*, 88-9.

Chapter 5 The Victorian Empire, Agricultural Depressions and Trade Unionism

li James Morris, *Heaven's Command, an Imperial Progress*, 133.

lii James Morris, ibid., 164.

liii James Morris, ibid., 149-50.

liv Pauline Ashridge, op.cit., 5.

lv Philip Marsden, *The Levelling Sea*, 269.

lvi G.E. Mingay, *Rural Life in Victorian England*, 19.

lvii Flora Thompson, *Lark Rise to Candleford*, 246.

lvii Pamela Horn, *Agricultural Trade Unionism and Emigration, 1872-1881* (The Historical Journal, xv, 1 (1972), pp.87-102).

lviii Ken Harris, *The Swanbourne Agricultural Workers' Strike of 1873*.

lix Pamela Horn, op.cit., 97.

lxi Pamela Horn, op.cit., 100-101.

lxii Owen Chadwick

lxiii G.E. Mingay, op. cit.

lxiv Article by Duncan White on *'The Dickens Boy'* by Tom Keneally in the Daily Telegraph on 28 August 2020.

lxv Flora Thompson, op.cit., 39-4.

Chapter 6 The Great Exodus, 1850-1914

lxvi Audrey M.Taylor, op.cit., 177.

lxvii Barrie Trinder (ed), *Victorian Banbury, Three Memoirs, Sarah Beesley 1812-1892, Thomas Ward Boss 1825-1903, Thomas Butler Gunn 1863* (Banbury Historical Society, Vol 33, 2013).

lxviii David Watts and Peter Barrington, *The Changing Faces of Bicester*, Book Four, 94-5.

lxix Rhonda Smith and the Butler family, Queensland, Australia.

lxx Michael Raymus Butler, *Oxfordshire to Taranaki, New Zealand* (Oxfordshire Family History, Vol 18 No.2 August 2004).

lxxi Don Chapman, *An Emigrant's Chronicle* (Oxford Mail, 28 March 1961).

lxxii Malcolm Harvey, Juniper, Oxon.

lxxiii *Addinsall Family History, 1640-1993, Savin and Freeman Families from Launton to Victoria.*

lxxiv John Freeman, *Letter to Bicester Herald*, 31 May 1867.

lxxv Tom McQuay and Duncan Waugh, *A Determined Emigrant* (Wychwoods Local History Society, no.11(1996), 58-59).

lxxvi Barry McKay, op.cit.

lxxvii Alfred Joy, *The Diary of Alfred Joy, 1853-54.* (OHC Pamphlett OXFO/325.2)

lxxviii Ken Harris, op.cit.

lxxix Paper re assisted emigrants to Quebec, 1853-54 (NRO PL01/564)

lxxx Poor Law Association standard form to raise £15, 12 November 1851 ((NRO G(K)300).

lxxxi Poor Law Association standard form to raise £15, 15 October 1852 (NRO G(K)301).

lxxxii Letter from John Simpson to Rev A.C.Neely, 16 February 1869 (NRO O17P/116).

lxxxiii Annie Saunders, and her Emigration from Warwickshire to Ontario (Our Warwickshire website).

lxxxiv Addinsall Family History, ibid.

lxxxv M.K.Ashby, op.cit., 89.

Chapter 7 Migrant Ports, Shipping and Passages

[lxxxvi] Kevin Brown, *Passages to the World*, 30.

[lxxxvii] William Plomer (ed), *Kilvert's Diary, 1870-1879, Selections from the Diary of the Rev. Francis Kilvert*, 181-3 (1944).

[lxxxviii] The Butler and Whitton families.

[lxxxix] Dr J.Blencowe, op.cit., 84-6.

[xc] Articles required by a labourer for the Cape, 1837 (CBS D/LE/H9/34).

[xci] Letter from Rev Brown of Pytchley, ibid.

[xcii] Memo of Great Linford parish, ibid.

[xciii] Expenses of Faulkners and party from Pytchley, ibid.

[xciv] Final list of expenses from Pytchley, ibid.

[xcv] Poor Law Authorisation form from Syresham, ibid.

[xcvi] Letter from John Simpson to the Rector of Stony Stratford, ibid.

[xcvii] Kershaw, op.cit., 120-1.

[xcviii] Kevin Brown, op.cit., 41.

[xcix] Kevin Brown, ibid., 38-40.

[c] Kevin Brown, ibid., 156.

[ci] Kevin Brown, ibid., 140.

[cii] Rachel Strachen and the Tackley Local History Group

[ciii] Kevin Brown, ibid., 140.

[civ] Kevin Brown, ibid., 136-8.

[cv] Stephen Guy, *From the Deep*, 4 May 2010 (Merseyside Maritime Museum blog).

[cvi] Stephen Guy, *The sinking of the Royal Charter*, 26 October 1859, ibid. (2009).

[cvii] Kevin Brown, op.cit., 145-6.

[cviii] Kevin Brown, ibid, 147-9.

[cix] Kevin Brown, ibid., 159.

[cx] Kevin Brown, ibid., 161-2.

[cxi] Kevin Brown, ibid., 169-70.

[cxii] Kevin Brown, ibid., 174-5.

[cxiii] *The Diary of Joseph Sams*, 58.

[cxiv] Westland, *Journal of John Hillary, emigrant to New Zealand*, 1879, 45.

[cxv] Kevin Brown, op.cit., 192.

Chapter 8 Diaries and Other Records of Emigrants

[cxvi] Tasmania State Library and Archive Service.

[cxvii] *The Diary of Alfred Joy, 1853-4*, ibid.

[cxviii] Rhonda Smith and the Butler family, Queensland, Australia.

Appendix 3 Cornish Emigration

[cxix] Philip Payton, *The Cornish Overseas, The epic story of the 'Great Emigration'* (2005).

Index

Abingdon, Earl of, 70
Adderbury, 29, 33
Addinsell, John, 75-76. 84
Adelaide, 52, 81
Agincourt, 15
agricultural depressions, 29, 31, 59-60, 76
agricultural labourers, 56, 60, 64, 67-68, 77, 86, 114, 117-118
Agricultural Trade Unionism, 60, 77
Akaroa, 20
Alberta, Canada, 17
Albert Dock, 85
Alcester, 50
America, 14-17, 33, 34, 37-38, 45, 47, 53, 64, 67, 82, 84, 85, 86, 89, 91, 92, 101, 105, 119, 123-125, 127
American War of Independence, 14
Amersham, 39
Anti-Corn Law League, 26
Arbuthnot, Col, 18
Arch, Joseph, 61-62, 64
Argentina, 72, 105
Artemisia, 18
Ascott-under-Wychwood, 61, 77, 114
Ashby, Joseph, 53, 84
Aahby, William, 53, 84
Ashton, 82, 91
Aston Rowant, 36
Atlantic, 17, 57, 92, 103
Atlantic, 104
Auckland, NZ, 20, 77, 104, 114
Austin, Reuben, 65
Australasia, 14-15, 57, 67
Australia, 14-20, 33, 34, 37-38, 41, 47, 52, 56-57, 59, 71, 75, 83, 84, 85, 92, 99, 101, 104, 105, 117, 119, 127
Australian Land & Emigration Co., 83
Austria, 103
Ava, 81
Aylesbury, 36, 39, 80
Aylesford, Earl of, 50, 82

Balfour Declaration, 19
Ballochmyle, 61, 64, 77
Ballarat, Victoria, 18
Bampton, 29, 36
Banbury, 26, 27, 29-31, 33, 48, 53, 70-71
Banbury Guardian, 70
Baptists, see Nonconformists,
Bathurst, NSW, 18, 41
Bathurst, S.Africa, 22
Bedford, Duke of, 79
Bedfordshire, 30
Beesley, Sarah, 71
Begbroke, 37, 107
Bendigo, Victoria, 18
Berkhamsted, 39, 79
Bible Christians, 63
Bicester, 25, 27, 30, 34, 72, 75
Bicester Advertiser, 60, 67, 117
Bicester Herald, 76
Bideford, 89, 127
Bidgoods of Oxford, 108
Birmingham, 50
Birmingham Bull Ring Riots, 25
blanket manufacture, 30, 37
Bledlow, 36
Blenheim Park, 70
Bletchley, 39
Bliss, Thomas, 30
Bliss, William, 30
Blisworth Tunnel, 44

Bloxham, 29, 33, 71
Bodicote, 33, 91
Boer Republics, 22
Boston, 102
Botany Bay, 13-14
Boulton, Matthew, 70
Brackley, 35, 45. 48
Bremen, 86
brewing & malting, 30-31
Brisbane, 14, 18, 19, 70, 73, 80, 104
Bristol, 24, 85, 89
British Columbia, 17, 119
British Empire, see Victorian Empire
Brogdens, 21, 64, 76-77
Broke, NSW, 15
Brown, Ford Madox, 98
Brougham, Lord, 55, 123, 124
Broughton, Northants, 48
Brownlow, Earl of, 39, 79
Brunel, Isambard, 37, 92
Buccleuch, Duke of, 42, 50, 80, 81
Buckingham, Duke of, 39, 79
Buckinghamshire, 30, 39-42, 69, 79-80
Buenos Aires, 72
Bun Penny, 58-59
Bunyan, John, 65-66
Burford, 29
Burghley, Stamford, 42
Burton Latimer, 42
Butler, Ellen, 110
Butler family, 15, 70, 73, 110, 112, 113
Butler, Charles, 73, 110, 113
Butler, Henry, 73, 89, 110 113
Butler, Hugh Ramsey, 111, 112
Butler, Joseph, 73, 89, 110

Butler, Ormand, 111, 112
Butler, Raymus, 72
Butler, Shirley, 112
Butler, Thomas, 73, 110, 112, 113
Butlin, Thomas, 45

Cachelet, 20
California, 71, 115, 119, 127
Cameron of Lochiel, 107
Canada, 33-34, 37, 38, 48, 53, 56, 60, 67-68, 71, 72, 75, 85, 89, 91, 92, 104, 105, 114, 1117, 119, 120, 123, 125, 127
Canada, Upper and Lower, 17, 55, 123
Canadian rebellion, 55, 123
Canterbury, NZ, 20, 64, 77, 105, 114
Canton, 48, 52, 73
Cape of Good Hope, 37, 48, 77, 104, 108
Cape Province, 22, 90, 127
Cape Town, 20, 22
Cardwell, N. Queensland, 110
Carington, Lord, 39, 79
Carter, Charles, 21, 22, 64, 76
Cartvale, 73-74
Cataraqui, 34, 35, 37, 38, 102, 103, 117
Cato Street conspiracy, 23
Chacombe, 33, 47, 70
chair making, 30
Charlbury, 29, 114
Charles Kerr, 52
Chartists, 21, 25-26
Cherwell Valley, 29, 30
Chesterton, 34, 38
Chetwynd, Lord, 25
Chiltern Hills,, 30, 39
China Tea Run, 18, 57
Chinnor, 36
Chipping Norton, 29, 30, 76
Christchurch, NZ, 20, 61, 75
Clanfield, 78
Claydon, 39, 71

Cobalt, N. Ontario, 83-84, 114
Coke-Smyth, J.R., 123
Collingwood, Melbourne, 109, 111
Colonial Land and Emigration Commissioners, 49, 67
Compton Verney, 50
Compton Wynyates, 50
Comte de Paris, 20
Congregationalists, see Nonconformists
Constance, 49, 91
convicts, 13-14, 18
Cook, Captain James, 13-14, 117
copper, 127, 128
Cornish emigration, 22, 65, 89, 127
Cornish Methodists, 128
Corn Laws, 23, 55, 117
Cospatrick, 77, 104, 117
Cottisford, 75
Coughton Court, 50
Cousin Jack, 127
Coventry, 49
Coventry Canal, 50
cricket, 20, 57
Cubbington, 83-84, 114, 117
Cuddesdon, 35, 78
Cunard, 92, 98
Cutty Sark, 57, 58

Daintree, Richard, 62
Darling Downs, 73
Dashwood, Sir Henry, 70, 79
Dashwood, Lady, 79
Daventry, 45, 81
David Scott, 52
Deddington, 29, 37, 70, 79
Demosthenes, 75
Derwent Water, 107
Devon, 67, 127
Dickens, Charles, 67
disasters, 101-104, 117
Dominions, 17-19
Donovan & Beckets, 90

Dorchester, 36, 90
Dorunda, 104
Douglas, 75
Droitwich, 71, 91,
Dunedin, NZ, 20, 79
Durham, Earl of, 55, 118, 123-125
Durham, Lady, 55, 123-125
Durham, Lady, 55, 123-125
Durham Report, 17, 55-56, 117, 118

East Anglia, 24
Eldridge, Captain, 102
East London, S.Africa, 22
Ellice, Alexander, 125
Ellice, Edward, 123, 125
Ellice, Edward 'Bear', 125
Ellice, Jane, 123, 125
emigration costs, 90-91
emigrant depots, 92, 98, 105
emigrants diaries & other records, 107-115
emigrant paintings. 99-101
Emperor, 41
Endeavour, 13
epidemic diseases, 104-106, 117
Epwell, 70
Europe, 20, 68, 85, 89
Exeter, Marquis of, 42, 80
Exmouth, 102
Eydon, 48
Eynsham, 36

Falmouth, 89, 127
farming, 23, 29, 39, 44, 50
Farthinghoe, 70
Featherstone, Dr Isaac, 21
female emigrants, 19
Finedon, 44-45
Finmere, 35, 41
First Fleet, 14
Fitzwilliam,The Hon George, 42, 80
Forth, 41
Foster, John, 85
Four Shires. 68, 117
Fowey, 89, 117

France, 20
Freeman, John, 75-76
French Canadians, 14, 17, 55, 123
Fremantle, Sir Thomas, 61, 80
Fringford. Oxon, 38, 70, 72, 89
Fringford, N. Queensland, 110, 112, 113
Fritwell, 31, 35, 38, 73
Fuller, Revd Thomas, 22

Geddington, 82
Gibraltar Bay, 104
Girdlestone, Canon, 67
Glasgow, 18
glove making, 30
Golden Jubilee, 59
Gold Rush, 17, 18, 22, 71, 99, 103, 109, 127
Grace, W.G., 20
Grafton, Duke of, 79
Grahamtrown, South Africa, 22
Grand Union Canal, 39, 44, 50
Gravesend, 52, 73, 78, 80, 89, 107
Great Britain, 109
Great Exodus, 26, 56, 57-84, 117
Great Haseley, 35, 38
Great Linford, 42, 91
Great Milton, 78
Great Ouse, 39
Greater Rollright, 60
Great Western, 92, 101
Great Western Steamship Company, see Guion
Greatworth with Westhorp, 48
Greenwood family, 119-120
Greenwood State Bank, 119, 120
Grey, Lord, 24
Grosse Ile, 17, 104

Guion, 92
Gulf of St Lawrence, 17, 102, 104
Gunn, Thomas, 71

Haggard, Rider, 29, 60
Hagley Park, Christchurch, NZ, 20
Halifax, Canada, 83
Hamburg, 86, 89
Hanwell, 71
Hawthorne, Melbourne, 110
health improvements, 58, 105-106
Henley-on-Thames, 31, 35
Hereford, Marquis of, 50, 82
Highland clearances, 104
High Wycombe, 30
Hillary, John, 92, 105
HMS Anson, 104
Hobart, Tasmania, 52, 107
Hobson's Bay, 108
Holloway, Chris, 62, 64, 79
Holton, 80
Hook Norton, 33
Hook Norton Brewery, 30
Hudson's Bay, 17
Hull, 85
Hunt Edmunds, 30

Iffley, 24
Inconstant, 125
Indus, 73
Inman Line, 92
Inverene, 114
Ireland, 17
Irish Catholics, 121
Irish emigrants, 104
ironstone mining, 44-45
Islip, 75

Jackson's Oxford Journal, 38
Jersey, Earl of, 70
Jewish emigrants, 89
Jordan, Henry, 18
Joy, Alfred, 78, 101, 108
Joy, Henrietta, 78, 108

Joyce, Ellen, 98-99
Junee, nr Katoomba, NSW, 72
Juniper Hill, see Lark Rise

Kettering, 45, 48
Kiddington, 37, 38
Kilvert, Francis, 85-86
Kingston-on-Thames, 109-110
King George the III, 13, 117
Kingham. 107
Kirtlington, 70
King Island, Australia, 38, 102
King's Sutton, 34, 38, 86, 90

lace making, 30, 39, 45
Lake Mills, Wisconsin, 119, 120
Lambton, Lord, see Earl of Durham
Langlois, Captain Jean, 20
Lark Rise, 59, 70, 89
Launceston, Tasmania, 41
Launton, 75
Leamington, 50, 62, 75, 83, 84,
Lee-on-Solent, 59
Legget, Joseph, 64
Leigh, Lord, 50, 82
Lindsey, Ontario, 115
Lisbon, 108
Little Bourton, 71
Liverpool, 20, 23, 34, 36, 38, 48, 70, 73, 85-89, 90, 98, 99, 102, 103, 104, 118, 127
Liverpool, Lord, 23
London, UK, 36, 52, 53, 85, 89, 127
Londonderry, 102
Lower Heyford, 27, 35, 75
Lysander, 91
Lyttelton, NZ, 105

Mackay, N. Queensland, 73, 110

Magnetic Island, N.
    Queensland, 73, 110
Mahomed Shah, 36
Makaretu,, 114
Manaia, NZ, 75
Manchester, 23
Manly, Spring Cove,
    Sydney, 105
Maori, 20
Marlborough, Duke of, 29,
    70
Mariner, 107
McConachie, Alexander, 15
Melbourne, , 18, 36, 37, 38,
    49, 52, 57, 71, 78, 80, 84,
    91, 102, 104, 105, 107, 108,
    109
Melbourne, Lord, 55, 124
Merchant Taylors School,
    Crosby, 89
Mermaid, 20
Mersey, River, 85, 99
Michigan, 127
Middleton Cheney, 70
Middleton Park, 70
Midlands, 24, 27, 29
Milthorpe, NSW, 41
Milton-under-Wychwood,
    61, 64, 77, 114
mining, 83, 114, 127, 128
Minster Lovell, 26
Mixbury, 30
Mollington, 27
Mongol, 62, 79
Montreal, 53, 91
Moonta, 127
Mordaunt, Sir Charles, 81
Moreton Bay, see Brisbane
Morley, 26
Muddy Creek, Victoria, 75,
    84
Murray Upper, N.
    Queensland, 110, 111,
    112

Napoleonic Wars, 23, 26, 30,
    117
Natal, 22

National Agricultural
    Labourers Union
    (NALU), 30, 61, 62, 64,
New Brunswick, 47
New England, 125
Newport rising, 25
New South Wales (NSW),
    14, 18, 52, 70, 72, 73, 105,
    127
New World, 35
New York,48, 72, 85, 90, 102,
    119, 124
New Zealand, 13-14, 17, 18,
    20, 21, 22, 53, 57, 59, 60,
    62, 63, 64, 76-77, 78, 80, 85,
    92, 104, 114, 117, 127
Nonconformists, 22, 65, 76,
    77, 84, 128
Norfolk Island, 14, 15, 16
Northampton,, 42, 44, 45
Northampton, Marquis of,
    81
Northamptonshire, 30, 39,
    42-49, 69, 80-82
Northern Queensland, 13,
    73, 74, 89
Northumberland, 105
North West Territories,
    Canada, 17, 67
Nottingham Castle, 24

Ocean Monarch, 102
O'Connor, Feargus, 25
Oithona, 84
O'Neil, Henry, 98
Orange Free State, 22
Ormandville, NZ, 114
Otago colony, NZ, 20
Otmoor, 24
Ottawa, 17, 61, 120,
Overstone, Lord, 39, 42, 79,
    80
Oxford, 27, 29, 31
Oxford Movement, 20
Oxford Bread Riots, 24
Oxford Canal. 37, 44, 60
Oxfordshire, 24, 27-38, 60,
    62, 69, 118, 128

Pacific, 13
Pacific, 102
Padstow, 89, 127
Palmer, Revd William, 41
Palmyra,41
passages, 20, 101, 118
Passenger Acts, 92, 105
Peel Island Q Station, 104
Peel, Sir Robert, 26, 50, 53, 82
penal colonies, 14
Penzance, 89, 127
Perth, Tasmania, 15
Peterborough, 42
Peterloo, 23
Picton, South Island, NZ, 76
Plug Riots, 26
plush, 29
Plymouth, 36, 53, 62, 64, 75,
    79, 85, 89, 92, 98, 105, 117
Poor Laws, 24, 25, 33, 49, 81-
    82, 117
Poor Law Unions, 31, 41, 117
population, 20, 22, 31, 32, 40,
    41, 43, 45, 50, 51, 70, 79-80,
    82-83
Port Arthur, Tasmania, 14
Port Elizabeth, South Africa,
    22
Port Phillip, see Melbourne
Port Jackson, NSW, 14
Port Stephens, NSW, 15
ports, migrant, 85-89
Possession Island, 13
Posthumous,49, 91
Potato Famine, 17, 104, 127

Pratley, Eli, 77
Primitive Methodists, see
    Nonconformists
Prince Edward Island, 125
Prince Regent, 15
Promised Land, 65, 67, 92,
    117, 119, 120
Pyrton, 35
Pytchley, 46, 49, 82, 90, 91

Quebec, 41, 71, 78, 81, 90, 91,
    104, 125

Queensland, 14, 18, 19, 60, 61, 62, 63, 70, 73, 78, 80, 98, 105, 117, 118
Queen Victoria, 18, 104, 105
Q Stations, 17, 104, 105

railways, 20, 21, 29, 39, 45, 58, 67, 76
Radnage, 80
Ragley, Alcester, 50
Ramsden, 70, 83
Ramsey, 80
Ratley, 70, 83
Red Jacket, 102
Reform Bill, 23, 24
Return of Owners Land, 29, 39, 42, 60, 68, 70, 79, 80-81, 82
Richardson, Edward, 42-43, 80
Ripa Island Q Station, NZ, 103
Risley, Revd William, 37
Rockhampton, Queensland, 73,
Rothschild, Baron L. N. de, 31, 79
Rothwell, 49
Rousham, 37, 38
Royal Albert, 33
Royal Charter, 103
Royal Dane, 73
Rugby, 50
Rushton, 49
Russell, Lord John, 55, 118, 124

Saint Anne, 34
Sams, Joseph, 105
Sarah, 52
Saskatchewan, Canada, 17
Saturday Review, 99
Saunders, Annie, 83-84, 114-115
Scimitar, 62, 79
Scottish Presbyterians, 128
Scotland, 18, 20
settlements, emigrant, 17-22

Sheffield, Tasmania, 65
shipping, 18, 57, 92-99,
Shipton-under-Wychwood, 77
Shipston-on-Stour, 53
shoemaking and leather working, 44
Shotteswell, 83
Shutford, 29
Sibford, 70
Sidmouth, Viscount, 23
Simons, John, 72
Simons, Thomas, 72,
Singleton, NSW, 15
Sisters, 71
Six Acts, 23
social unrest, 23-24
Somes Island, Q Station, Wellington, 75, 105
Souldern, 30, 70
South Africa, 17, 22, 127
South America, 59
South Australia, 18, 22, 46, 49, 52, 65, 90-92, 127
Southampton, 81, 84, 85, 86, 89, 92
South Leigh, 78
South Newington, 33, 71
Speenhamland System, 24
Spencer, Earl, 42, 80
Spurgeon, Charles, 65-66
SS Great Britain, 57, 59
Staniland, Charles, 98, 100
Stanton Harcourt, 78
Stanton St John, 35, 90
Star of the West, 99
Statesman, 34
steamships, 52, 89, 101, 117
Steel, Michael, 107
Steel, William, 107
Steeple Aston, 79
Steeple Barton, 37
St Helena, Moreton Bay, 105
St Ives, 89, 127
St Lawrence River, 125
Stockton, 50
Stokr Bruerne, 44
Stoke Lyne, 30, 35, 38

Stonesfield, 37, 38
Stonehouse, 75
Strathfieldsaye, 52
straw plaiting, 45
Suez Canal, 57, 92
Swanbourne, nr Winslow, 61, 80
Swan River Colony, see Western Australia
Swing Riots, 23
Sydney, 15, 20, 34, 52, 71, 83, 98, 105
Syresham, 81-82, 91

Tackley, 37, 38, 102
Tadmarton, 34
Tahiti, 13
Tasmania, 14, 15, 16, 18, 26, 37, 38, 41, 62, 65, 66, 107,
Taylor, Henry, 62, 64, 79
Taynton, 114
Templar, 34
Terry family, 81,
Terry, Joseph, 15
Terry, Richard (the elder), 15
Terry, Richard, (the younger), 15,
Tew Park, 70
Thame, 29, 35
Thames, River, 39, 50, 99
Thermopylae, 57
Thetia, 81
Thomas Harrison, 78, 107
Thompson, Flora, 70
Thompson, Henry Basil, 70
Three Graces, Liverpool, 86
Throckmorton, Sir N.W., 50, 82
Ticonderigo, 104
Timms, Edwin, 75
Timms. Emma, 70
Timms, Frank, 70, 75
Tingewick, 41
Tornado, 20
Toronto, 115
Towcester, 45, 81
Townsville, N, Queensland, 73, 104, 110

transportation, 13, 14, 15, 23, 24, 83
Transvaal, 22
Trevelyan, Charles, 55
trucking, 38
Truro, 89, 127
Twyford, Bucks, 41
Tysoe, 53, 62, 84

United States, see America
Utopia, 104

Vancouver, 115, 119
Vancouver Island, 17, 119
Van Diemen's Land, see Tasmania
Verney, Sir Henry, 39
Victoria, Australia, 18, 75, 83
Victoria, 33
Victorian Empire, 55-56, 117, 118
Virginius, 104
Vogel, Sir Julius, 20, 21

Waddesdon, 39, 71
wages, 52
Waitangi, Treaty of, 20
Wakefield, Edward, 18
Warkworth, 45
Warmington, 70
Warren, 34
Warwick Castle, 50
Warwick, Earl of, 50, 82
Warwickshire, 49-53, 62, 69, 82-84
weavers, 29
Wellesbourne, 61
Wellingborough, 45
Wellington, NZ, 20, 73, 76
Wesleyans, see Nonconformists
Western Australia, 14, 18
West Indies, 14, 125
Westland, 105
White Star Line, 20, 92
Whittingham, NSW, 15
Whitton, George, 89

William Braham, 48
Williamstown, Melbourne, 108
Winnipeg, 75
Witney, 29, 30, 37, 78
Willoughby De Broke, Lord, 50, 82
Woburn Abbey, 79
women, 19, 29, 52, 61, 98, 105, 117
Wolverton, 39
Woodstock, 30, 38
Woodville Settlement, 114
wool and hides, 18, 29
Woolwich, 15
Wootton, 38, 62, 63, 79
Woughton, 42
Wrench, William, 29
Wroxton, 71
Wychwoods, 64, 76, 104
Wytham, Oxford, 70

Yabbon, Murray Upper, 110
Young, Arthur, 55